The Easy
BLACKSTONE
GRIDDLE

Cookbook for Beginners

Delicious and Juicy Recipes with Expert Tips and Tricks for Every Occasion—
From Sizzling Burgers and Steaks to Fluffy Pancakes and Beyond

Alvin Hernandez

Table of Contents

INTRODUCTION

.In the realm of outdoor cooking, the Blackstone griddle has carved out its own niche, captivating both seasoned chefs and casual backyard cooks. This remarkable appliance has revolutionized the way we approach griddling, offering a versatile cooking surface that brings the joys of outdoor dining to your backyard, patio, or campsite. If you're ready to explore a new world of culinary possibilities, this cookbook is your ultimate guide to mastering the art of griddling.

The Allure of the Blackstone Griddle

At its core, the Blackstone griddle embodies convenience and innovation. With its expansive cooking surface, it allows you to prepare multiple dishes at once, making it perfect for family gatherings, parties, or simply enjoying a meal with friends. Imagine sizzling burgers, perfectly seared vegetables, and fluffy pancakes all at your fingertips, cooked to perfection in a matter of minutes. The griddle's ability to distribute heat evenly ensures that everything from meats to delicate fish cooks consistently, making it a favorite among culinary enthusiasts.

What truly sets the Blackstone griddle apart is its adaptability. Whether you're a fan of breakfast classics, hearty dinners, or international cuisines, the griddle can handle it all. This book is designed to inspire your culinary creativity, helping you to explore a diverse range of recipes that highlight the unique capabilities of the Blackstone griddle.

Elevating Outdoor Cooking

Cooking outdoors is about more than just the food; it's about the experience. The Blackstone griddle turns any gathering into an occasion, inviting friends and family to come together around the grill. As you fire up your griddle, the enticing aromas of sizzling food fill the air, creating an inviting atmosphere that encourages conversation and laughter. This cookbook celebrates that spirit of togetherness, offering recipes that are meant to be shared and enjoyed.

From casual weekend breakfasts to festive dinner parties, the Blackstone griddle provides an excellent platform for culinary exploration. Its ability to accommodate a variety of cooking techniques—grilling, sautéing, and even frying—makes it the ultimate outdoor cooking companion. This versatility opens the door to a world of flavors and dishes, allowing you to step outside traditional cooking boundaries and create unforgettable meals.

A Gateway to Culinary Creativity

One of the most exciting aspects of using a Blackstone griddle is the freedom it offers in the kitchen. Unlike traditional cooking methods, griddling encourages experimentation. With its wide cooking surface, you can easily prepare multiple dishes simultaneously, allowing for flavor combinations and innovative presentations that elevate your meals to a new level.

This cookbook is packed with recipes that challenge you to think outside the box. You'll discover how to whip up everything from classic breakfast favorites to exotic international dishes, each tailored for the griddle. Imagine creating a savory Spanish paella right on your outdoor griddle or serving up fresh, grilled stir-fry packed with colorful vegetables and bold flavors. The possibilities are endless, and each recipe is an opportunity to ignite your passion for cooking.

Cooking for Everyone

The Blackstone griddle is not just for the culinary elite; it's for everyone. This cookbook is designed with cooks of all skill levels in mind, whether you're a beginner eager to learn or an experienced griller looking to expand your repertoire. The straightforward instructions, helpful tips, and easy-to-follow recipes ensure that anyone can become a griddle master in no time.

Cooking is a universal language, and the Blackstone griddle makes it accessible to all. Invite your children to join you in the kitchen, teaching them the fundamentals of cooking while creating lasting memories. With its user-friendly design and versatility, the griddle empowers families to come together and explore the joys of cooking as a team.

Embracing a Healthier Lifestyle

Another significant advantage of using the Blackstone griddle is its potential for healthier cooking. By using less oil and focusing on fresh ingredients, you can prepare delicious meals that are not only satisfying but also nutritious. This cookbook emphasizes the importance of incorporating whole foods into your diet, showcasing recipes that celebrate the bounty of fresh vegetables, lean proteins, and flavorful herbs and spices.

From vibrant vegetable stir-fries to grilled fish tacos, the Blackstone griddle allows you to create meals that nourish both body and soul. As you explore these recipes, you'll find that healthy eating doesn't have to be boring or restrictive. With the right ingredients and techniques, you can savor meals that are both delicious and good for you.

Your Culinary Adventure Awaits

As you embark on this culinary journey, remember that cooking is about exploration and joy. The Blackstone griddle is your canvas, inviting you to paint your meals with bold flavors and creative presentations. Each recipe in this cookbook is an opportunity to express your culinary style, whether it's a classic dish reimagined or a brand-new creation born from your imagination.

Get ready to embrace the joys of outdoor cooking with the Blackstone griddle. With this cookbook in hand, you'll discover that griddling is not just a cooking method; it's a way to connect with food, friends, and family. So fire up your griddle, gather your loved ones, and let the culinary adventure begin! Happy cooking!

Chapter 1 Breakfasts

BBQ Brisket Breakfast Tacos

These delicious breakfast tacos bring together the perfect mix of BBQ, breakfast, and taco flavors. Using leftover brisket, this recipe transforms it into a mouthwatering meal with crispy edges and tender bites. Cooking it on the Blackstone griddle enhances the flavors, making each bite unforgettable. Pair the brisket with fluffy scrambled eggs, melted cheese, and a bit of heat for the ultimate breakfast taco experience.

Makes 2 servings

Ingredients:

◄ 2 ounces (56 g) smoked brisket, leftover

◄ 4 eggs

◄ 4 teaspoons (20 ml) half-and-half

◄ Pinch of salt and black pepper

◄ 1 tablespoon (14 g) unsalted butter

◄ 2 small flour tortillas

◄ 1 ounce (28 g) shredded Mexican cheese

◄ 4 teaspoons (20 ml) hot sauce

◄ 1 teaspoon parsley or cilantro flakes for garnish

1. Preheat your Blackstone griddle to medium heat and lightly oil the surface. This will allow you to cook everything at the same time.
2. Slice the brisket into small, bite-sized chunks and place it on the griddle. Stir occasionally to ensure it heats evenly and crisps up nicely. This should take about 5 to 6 minutes.
3. In a bowl, whisk together the eggs, half-and-half, salt, and pepper. Mix until combined and set aside.
4. Lower the heat on a separate side of the griddle to medium-low. Melt the butter and spread it evenly. Pour the egg mixture onto the griddle, using a spatula to gently move the eggs around until they're fully scrambled but still soft. This process should take about 5 to 6 minutes.
5. While the eggs cook, place the tortillas on the hot part of the griddle to warm them up for about 2 minutes per side.
6. Once everything is ready, divide the brisket and eggs evenly between the two tortillas. Sprinkle with cheese, drizzle hot sauce, and garnish with parsley or cilantro flakes. Enjoy immediately.

Ham and Spinach Omelet with Melty Colby Jack

This protein-packed omelet is a simple yet flavorful dish perfect for any meal of the day. The combination of savory ham, fresh spinach, and melty Colby Jack cheese creates a satisfying bite every time. Using the Blackstone griddle adds a unique texture to the omelet, making it ideal for serving one or even scaling up for a crowd. With minimal ingredients, each flavor truly shines in this easy-to-follow recipe.

Makes 1 serving.

Ingredients:

◄ ½ cup (110 g) diced ham

◄ ½ cup (15 g) baby spinach

◄ 1 tablespoon (14 g) unsalted butter

◄ Pinch of salt and ground black pepper

◄ 3 large eggs, scrambled

◄ ¾ cup (84 g) shredded Colby Jack cheese

◄ Hot sauce or salsa, for serving

◄ Equipment: 8-inch (20-cm) Pancake/Omelet Mold

1. Begin by heating your griddle to medium-low and lightly oiling the surface to prevent sticking.

2. Once the griddle is hot, add the diced ham and cook for 4 to 5 minutes, stirring occasionally until it starts to brown. Toss the baby spinach into the ham and stir for about 30 seconds, just until the spinach wilts. Move this mixture to the side of the griddle.

3. Position the 8-inch omelet mold on the griddle, ensuring both the mold and griddle are sprayed with cooking oil. Melt the butter inside the mold.

4. Season the scrambled eggs with a pinch of salt and pepper, then slowly pour the eggs into the mold. Let them cook undisturbed for 2 minutes.

5. Add the ham and spinach mixture to one half of the omelet and top that side with the shredded Colby Jack cheese.

6. After about 5 minutes, once the eggs have firmed up and are slightly golden on the bottom, carefully remove the mold using a rubber spatula to loosen the edges.

7. Gently fold the omelet in half, flipping it to ensure the cheese melts and the egg is fully cooked. Serve immediately with hot sauce or salsa for an extra kick.

Mak's Easy Breakfast Muffins

We call these breakfast sandwiches "MakMuffins" in honor of my daughter, Mak. They are quick, simple, and perfect for recreating that fast-food classic at home—but even better! Using the Blackstone griddle's ample space and multiple cooking zones, you can have these breakfast sandwiches ready in no time.

Makes 4 servings

Ingredients:

- ◀ 4 eggs
- ◀ Salt and ground black pepper
- ◀ 4 pre-formed sausage patties (2 ounces [56 g] each)
- ◀ 4 English muffins, sliced
- ◀ 4 slices American cheese
- ◀ Special Equipment: 4 silicone egg rings

1. Preheat your Blackstone griddle to medium heat across all burners. Place the silicone egg rings on the griddle and spray them lightly with canola oil. Crack an egg into each ring and stir to scramble. Season each egg with a pinch of salt and pepper. Cook for about 3 to 4 minutes, until the top of the egg starts to set, then remove the rings and flip the eggs for another 2 minutes.

2. While the eggs are cooking, place the sausage patties directly onto the griddle. Sprinkle each with black pepper and flip every minute until fully cooked, about 6 minutes total.

3. As the eggs and sausages cook, toast the cut sides of the English muffins on the griddle. After roughly 3 minutes, the muffins should be golden and crispy.

4. Once everything is cooked, assemble each MakMuffin by layering the bottom half of an English muffin with an egg, a slice of American cheese, and a sausage patty. Finish with the top half of the muffin. Serve these easy, homemade breakfast sandwiches warm and enjoy!

Mak's Chocolate Chip Brioche French Toast Delight

During Thanksgiving week, we always enjoy more breakfasts with the entire family gathered, and sweet treats are the top requests. This dish remains one of my wife's favorites—maybe it's the chocolate that makes it so special! This recipe is perfect for satisfying sweet cravings with a delicious twist.

Makes 8 servings

Ingredients:

- ◀ 1 teaspoon ground cinnamon
- ◀ ¼ teaspoon ground nutmeg
- ◀ 2 tablespoons (30 g) sugar
- ◀ 4 tablespoons (57 g) unsalted butter
- ◀ 4 large eggs
- ◀ ¼ cup (60 ml) milk
- ◀ ½ teaspoon vanilla extract
- ◀ 8 slices chocolate chip brioche bread (or substitute challah or white bread)
- ◀ ½ cup (120 ml) maple syrup, warmed
- ◀ 5 ounces (141 g) semi-sweet chocolate chips
- ◀ 4 large strawberries, sliced
- ◀ 4 tablespoons (30 g) powdered sugar

1. Preheat your griddle to medium heat and apply a thin layer of oil to prevent sticking. In a small bowl, mix together the cinnamon, nutmeg, and sugar. Set aside for later use.
2. Melt the butter on the griddle, spreading it evenly across the surface with a spatula to create a smooth, buttery layer.
3. In a shallow dish, whisk the cinnamon-sugar mixture together with the eggs, milk, and vanilla extract. Dip each slice of the chocolate chip brioche into the egg mixture, making sure both sides are fully coated.
4. Place the dipped bread slices onto the buttered griddle. Cook for about 6 minutes, flipping each slice every minute until they turn golden brown and crisp on the outside.
5. Serve the French toast warm, topped with maple syrup, semi-sweet chocolate chips, fresh strawberry slices, and a generous dusting of powdered sugar. Enjoy this sweet breakfast indulgence!

Chorizo & Egg Burrito Bliss

There's nothing quite like seeing a big, melty, cheesy burrito that makes your day better. Burritos are versatile and can be enjoyed for breakfast, lunch, dinner, or even dessert. We made these chorizo and egg burritos for dinner, and the flavors turned out incredible. Chorizo's bold spices add a rich depth to every bite, making it a standout ingredient.

Makes 2 servings

Ingredients:

- 12 ounces (340 g) chorizo
- ½ medium white onion, julienned
- ½ green bell pepper, julienned
- ½ yellow bell pepper, julienned
- 4 eggs
- 4 teaspoons (20 ml) half-and-half
- Salt and ground black pepper, divided
- 1 tablespoon (14 g) unsalted butter
- 2 large (12-inch [30-cm]) flour tortillas
- ½ cup (57 g) shredded Mexican cheese
- 3 tablespoons (45 ml) cilantro lime crema or salsa, for serving

1. Preheat the griddle to medium heat and apply a light layer of oil. If your chorizo has a casing, remove it. Break up the chorizo on the griddle using a spatula and cook it for 6 to 7 minutes, stirring occasionally. When it turns a deep brown color, push it to the side to keep warm.
2. Add the julienned onion and bell peppers to the area with the leftover chorizo drippings. Sauté the vegetables for about 5 minutes until softened.
3. In a bowl, whisk together the eggs, half-and-half, a pinch of salt, and black pepper.
4. Lower the heat on one side of the griddle to medium-low. Add the butter and spread it across the surface. Pour the egg mixture onto the griddle, using your spatula to gently drag the eggs as they start to cook. After about 6 minutes, once the eggs are cooked to your liking, fold them and move them to the side to keep warm.
5. Clean off the center of the griddle, reapply a light coat of oil, and heat the tortillas for 1 minute per side until they are soft and warm.
6. Assemble the burritos by placing ¼ cup of shredded cheese in the center of each tortilla. Add half of the eggs, half of the chorizo, and half of the sautéed veggies on top.
7. Roll the burritos tightly, folding the ends inward. Once rolled, place them back on the griddle, seam side down, and cook until browned on both sides, about 3 minutes per side.
8. Slice the burritos in half and serve with cilantro lime crema or your favorite salsa. For the perfect cheese pull, let the burrito rest for a minute before separating the halves. Enjoy!

Fluffy Buttermilk Pancake Stackers

A tall stack of buttermilk pancakes always brings a smile, especially when topped with melting butter and maple syrup dripping down the sides. This classic breakfast is perfect for any occasion, and now you can make it right at home, channeling your inner short-order cook!

Makes 4 servings

Ingredients:

- 2 cups (250 g) all-purpose flour
- 3 tablespoons (45 g) sugar
- 1½ teaspoon (7 g) baking powder
- 1½ teaspoon (7 g) baking soda
- 1¼ teaspoon (7 g) kosher salt
- 2½ cups (600 ml) buttermilk
- 2 large eggs
- 3 tablespoons (42 g) unsalted butter, melted, plus more for serving
- 4 tablespoons (60 ml) vegetable or canola oil, for the griddle, divided
- ½ cup (120 ml) maple syrup, warmed, for serving

1. In a bowl, whisk together the flour, sugar, baking powder, baking soda, and kosher salt. Create a well in the center of the dry mixture and pour in the buttermilk, crack in the eggs, and add the melted butter. Starting in the center, whisk everything together, gradually incorporating the dry ingredients. Do not overmix; it's okay if the batter is slightly lumpy.
2. Cover the bowl and let the mixture sit at room temperature for about 30 minutes. This resting time allows the buttermilk to activate and gives you fluffier pancakes.
3. As the batter rests, preheat the griddle on low heat for 5 minutes. Add 1 tablespoon (15 ml) of oil to the griddle, then increase the heat to medium-low. Use a measuring cup to ladle ⅓ cup (80 ml) of the batter onto the griddle for each pancake. Be careful not to overcrowd the pancakes as they cook.
4. When bubbles start to appear on the surface and the bottoms are golden brown (about 2 to 4 minutes), flip the pancakes. Cook the other side for another 1 to 2 minutes, until lightly browned. Remove the pancakes and place them on a warming rack on the griddle to keep warm while you finish cooking the rest.
5. Stack the pancakes as high as you like, topping them with a generous pat of butter and drizzling with warm maple syrup. Enjoy this fluffy, buttery delight!

Melanie's Chorizo Migas Fiesta

I named this dish after my wife Melanie, as she can never resist migas when they're on the menu—especially the veggie version! The crunch from the tortilla strips adds a texture and flavor that's hard to beat. Whether you go for chorizo or soyrizo for a vegetarian twist, this dish is packed with bold flavors and satisfying bites.

Makes 2 servings

Ingredients:

- ◀ 9 ounces (255 g) chorizo (or substitute soyrizo for vegetarian)
- ◀ 6 large eggs
- ◀ 2 tablespoons (30 ml) cilantro lime crema (or substitute half-and-half)
- ◀ Pinch of salt and ground black pepper
- ◀ 1 tablespoon (14 g) unsalted butter
- ◀ 1 ounce (28 g) tortilla strips (or substitute lightly crushed tortilla chips)
- ◀ 3 ounces (85 g) shredded Monterey Jack cheese
- ◀ 4 small flour or corn tortillas
- ◀ 1 large avocado, diced
- ◀ 1 (14-ounce [392-g]) can fire-roasted diced tomatoes, drained
- ◀ 1 bunch cilantro, chopped
- ◀ 1 tablespoon (4 g) cotija cheese
- ◀ Salsa or hot sauce, for serving

1. Preheat the griddle to medium heat and lightly oil the surface. Remove the chorizo from its casing if necessary, and break it apart on the griddle. Stir occasionally, cooking for about 6 to 8 minutes until browned, then set aside to keep warm.
2. In a bowl, whisk together the eggs, cilantro lime crema (or half-and-half), salt, and black pepper.
3. Lower the heat on the other side of the griddle to medium-low. Melt the butter and spread it across the surface. Pour the egg mixture onto the griddle, using the spatula to gently drag the eggs as they begin to cook. As the eggs solidify, add most of the tortilla strips into the eggs, saving a few for garnish.
4. Cook the eggs to your desired doneness, around 6 minutes. Fold them gently and set aside, topping the eggs with the shredded Monterey Jack cheese to let it melt.
5. Warm the tortillas on the griddle for about a minute on each side until soft and heated through.
6. Time to assemble the migas! In two bowls, divide the eggs, topping each with half the chorizo, diced avocado, and a spoonful of the fire-roasted tomatoes. Garnish with chopped cilantro, reserved tortilla strips, and a sprinkle of cotija cheese.
7. Serve with warm tortillas and your favorite salsa or hot sauce on the side. Enjoy this flavorful, crunchy breakfast with a kick!

Chapter 2 Delicious Mexican Tacos

Crunchy Beef Tacos with Zesty Chipotle Sauce

Nothing brings me back to childhood quite like crispy tacos. They were a weekly favorite in our house, and their versatility makes them a go-to for busy weeknights. The combination of crunchy shells, seasoned beef, and fresh toppings creates a meal that's easy to love and quick to make. Perfect for any day of the week!

Makes 12 servings

Ingredients:

◄ 1 pound (454 g) 90/10 ground beef

◄ 4 tablespoons (20 g) taco seasoning

◄ 3 ounces (85 g) flame-roasted diced green chiles

◄ 12 crispy corn taco shells

◄ 2 ounces (56 g) shredded Mexican cheese

◄ Shredded lettuce

◄ 1 (10-ounce [283-g]) can diced tomatoes, drained

◄ 1½ cups (360 ml) creamy chipotle sauce

◄ Spanish rice and refried beans, for serving

1. Heat your griddle to medium-high and lightly oil the surface. Once it's hot, add the ground beef and break it apart with a spatula. After about 5 minutes, stir in the taco seasoning and mix well. Continue cooking the beef, stirring frequently, for 8 to 10 minutes until it's fully browned.
2. When the beef is cooked through, stir in the flame-roasted green chiles. Turn off the heat but leave the beef on the griddle to stay warm.
3. Fill each crispy taco shell with a portion of the seasoned beef mixture. Top the tacos with shredded Mexican cheese, lettuce, diced tomatoes, and a drizzle of creamy chipotle sauce.
4. Serve the tacos alongside Spanish rice and refried beans for a complete meal. Enjoy these crispy, flavorful tacos any night of the week!

Grilled Salmon & Shrimp Tacos with Lime Crema

The Adventure Ready 22-inch (56-cm) Blackstone is our go-to for road trips, making it easy to whip up meals wherever we are. With a few tortillas, proteins, and veggies, you can enjoy quick, flavorful tacos anywhere. These salmon and shrimp tacos were prepared on the back porch of a lake house overlooking Lake Hamilton in Arkansas, but you can recreate them on any Blackstone, no matter the location.

Makes 6 servings

Ingredients:

- 3 (5-ounce [141-g]) skinless pink Atlantic salmon fillets
- 4 tablespoons (60 ml) olive oil
- 3 tablespoons (15 g) Blackstone Tequila Lime seasoning (or your favorite southwest seasoning), divided
- ½ pound (226 g) raw peeled and deveined shrimp
- 6 fajita-sized raw flour tortillas
- 1 (8-ounce [226-g]) package shredded tricolored coleslaw
- Salsa or your favorite crema sauce
- Quartered limes and chopped cilantro, for garnish

1. Start by patting the salmon fillets dry with a paper towel to remove any excess moisture, which ensures a better sear. Drizzle olive oil on all sides of each fillet and season generously with about a teaspoon of Tequila Lime seasoning on each side.
2. Repeat the same process with the shrimp—pat dry, lightly oil, and season with the remaining Tequila Lime seasoning.
3. Preheat the griddle to medium-high heat and apply a light layer of cooking spray. Place the raw flour tortillas on the griddle and cook for about 2 minutes, or until they start to bubble. Flip them and cook for another 2 to 3 minutes until light brown spots appear on both sides. Remove the tortillas from the griddle and keep them warm in a tortilla warmer or between two plates.
4. Add the seasoned salmon fillets to the griddle and cook for 3 to 4 minutes undisturbed. Flip the fillets when they have a nice sear and blackened finish, then cook for another 3 to 4 minutes. Break the salmon into bite-sized pieces, checking for doneness. When done, set the salmon aside on a cooler part of the griddle.
5. Scrape the griddle clean and reapply a light layer of cooking spray. Add the shrimp to the griddle and cook for about 90 seconds before flipping. Cook for another 90 seconds, or until the shrimp are pink, no longer translucent, and curled. Combine the shrimp and salmon together on the griddle.
6. Now it's time to assemble your tacos! On each tortilla, place about ½ ounce (14 g) of shredded coleslaw, followed by a mix of shrimp and salmon. Top with salsa or crema, and garnish with a squeeze of lime and a sprinkle of chopped cilantro. Serve immediately and enjoy!

Spicy Beef Birria Tacos with Rich Consommé

This recipe might take a little extra time and equipment, but the result is worth every bit of effort. Spicy beef combined with melty cheese and crispy tortillas, served with a rich, flavorful birria consommé, makes for an unforgettable taco experience. Traditionally from the Jalisco region of Mexico, birria is often made with goat meat, but this beef version is just as delicious.

Makes 12–24 tacos

Ingredients:

Beef:
- 4 pounds (1.8 kg) beef sirloin tip roast, cut into quarters
- 2 tablespoons (14 g) Meat Church Holy Voodoo seasoning (or your favorite spicy beef seasoning)

Birria Consommé:
- 4 cups (960 ml) beef broth
- 6 dried California chiles, seeds and stems removed
- 6 dried adobo chiles, seeds and stems removed
- 3 dried chiles de árbol, seeds and stems removed
- 1 (7-ounce [199-g]) can chipotle peppers in adobo sauce
- 2 cloves garlic, minced
- 1 tablespoon (6 g) dried oregano flakes
- 1 tablespoon (6 g) cumin
- 1 tablespoon (5 g) coriander
- 1 tablespoon (5 g) cayenne
- 1 tablespoon (7 g) Meat Church Holy Voodoo seasoning
- 1 cinnamon stick
- 1 bay leaf

Assembly:
- 24 taco-sized corn tortillas (white or yellow)
- 20 ounces (566 g) Oaxaca cheese, shredded
- 2 heads cilantro, chopped
- Salsa or your favorite crema sauce

- 1 (14-ounce [392-g]) can diced tomatoes, drained
- 2 medium white or red onions, chopped (divided)
- 1 cup (128 g) sliced baby carrots

- Quartered limes and chopped cilantro, for garnish
- Special Equipment:
- Instant Pot or Pressure Cooker

Instructions:

1. Preheat your griddle to high heat and lightly oil the surface. If using a smaller Blackstone (28-inch/71-cm), set all burners to high. For larger models, the middle burners set to high will do.
2. Season the beef sirloin tip roast quarters generously with Meat Church Holy Voodoo seasoning. Let the beef rest on the counter as the griddle heats up.
3. Once the griddle is hot, sear each side of the beef for about 60 seconds to create a caramelized crust. After searing, remove the beef from the heat and let it rest.
4. To prepare the birria consommé, bring the beef broth to a boil in a medium-sized pot. Add all the dried chiles (with seeds and stems removed), chipotle peppers, garlic, oregano, cumin, coriander, cayenne, Meat Church Holy Voodoo seasoning, cinnamon stick, and bay leaf. Stir to combine. Once boiling, reduce heat and let the broth simmer for 30 minutes until the chiles soften. Remove the cinnamon stick after 10 minutes.
5. After simmering, add the diced tomatoes to the broth and stir. Remove the bay leaf, then blend the broth in batches until smooth (2-3 minutes per batch). Pour the blended broth into an Instant Pot or pressure cooker. Add a quarter of the chopped onions, the sliced carrots, and the seared beef. Add water to cover the beef.
6. Secure the lid of the Instant Pot and set it to high pressure. Cook for 55 minutes. After cooking, safely release the pressure and remove the beef. Shred the beef with forks until it falls apart.
7. To assemble the tacos, keep the consommé nearby. Set the griddle to medium heat and lightly oil it. Dip each corn tortilla into the birria broth using tongs, then place them on the griddle. After a minute, flip the tortillas and top each one with shredded beef, Oaxaca cheese, cilantro, and chopped onions from the broth.
8. Fold the tacos in half and ladle a little consommé over them. Let the tacos cook for 3 to 4 minutes per side, flipping occasionally until the cheese melts and the tortillas crisp.
9. Repeat the process until all tacos are made. Serve with a side of consommé for dipping, garnished with extra cilantro and onions if desired. Enjoy these flavorful, crispy birria tacos!

Sweet Corn Tamale Cakes with Spicy Southwestern Sauce

With my wife being vegetarian, I'm always on the hunt for tasty and creative veggie dishes, and these tamale cakes hit the spot. The sweetness of the corn contrasts beautifully with the spicy and savory flavors, making it a perfect meal. Inspired by a restaurant appetizer, these tamale cakes are hearty enough to be a full entrée.

Makes 2 servings (3 corn cakes each)

Ingredients:

Southwestern Sauce:
- ½ cup (120 ml) mayonnaise
- 1 teaspoon white vinegar
- 1 teaspoon water
- 1 teaspoon sugar
- ½ teaspoon chili powder
- ¼ teaspoon paprika
- ⅛ teaspoon cayenne pepper
- ¼ teaspoon onion powder
- ⅛ teaspoon garlic powder

Pico de Gallo:
- 1 cup (160 g) white onion, finely chopped
- 1 jalapeño, ribs and seeds removed, finely chopped
- ¼ cup (60 ml) lime juice
- ¼ teaspoon sea salt, plus more to taste
- 1½ pounds (680 g) ripe red tomatoes, chopped
- 1 cup (16 g) fresh cilantro, chopped (divided), plus extra for garnish

Corn Cake:
- 3 cups (462 g) frozen sweet corn, divided
- 6 tablespoons (90 g) sugar
- ¼ teaspoon salt
- 1 cup (228 g) unsalted butter, softened
- 4 tablespoons (32 g) all-purpose flour
- 1 cup (125 g) corn masa harina flour
- 4 tablespoons (60 ml) olive oil

Garnish:
- 16 ounces (454 g) tomatillo salsa verde, warmed
- 2 tamale corn husks (optional)
- 16 ounces (454 g) sour cream, to taste
- 1 avocado, diced
- Cilantro, chopped for garnish

Instructions:

1. Prepare the Southwestern Sauce: In a small bowl, mix the mayonnaise, white vinegar, water, sugar, chili powder, paprika, cayenne, onion powder, and garlic powder until well combined. Transfer to a squeeze bottle and refrigerate until needed.
2. Make Pico de Gallo: In a large bowl, combine the chopped onion, jalapeño, lime juice, sea salt, tomatoes, and half of the cilantro. Stir well and chill until ready to serve.
3. Prepare the Corn Cake Mixture: Pulse 1 cup (154 g) of the frozen corn in a food processor until coarsely pureed. In a large bowl, mix the pureed corn with sugar, salt, and softened butter until combined.
4. Add Dry Ingredients: Stir in the all-purpose flour and masa harina flour. Mix well until there are no visible streaks of flour. Fold in the remaining 2 cups (308 g) of frozen corn kernels.
5. Form the Cakes: Use a ½-cup (120-ml) measuring cup to portion out the corn mixture. Shape each portion into 3-inch (8-cm) wide patties. If the mixture is too dry, add a tablespoon or two of water to help bind. Place patties on a parchment-lined baking sheet.
6. Cook the Cakes: Preheat your griddle to medium-low heat and drizzle olive oil on the surface. Once heated, carefully transfer the corn cakes from the parchment paper to the griddle. Cook for 5-8 minutes per side, until both sides are golden brown. Remove from heat.
7. Warm the Salsa: Heat the tomatillo salsa in a microwave-safe bowl for 1 to 2 minutes until warmed through.
8. Plate the Tamale Cakes: Lay a tamale corn husk flat on two plates (optional for presentation). Spoon about ½ cup (120 ml) of the warmed tomatillo salsa onto each plate. Place three corn cakes on each plate.
9. Add Toppings: Top each tamale cake with a dollop of sour cream, a generous serving of pico de gallo, diced avocado, and chopped cilantro.
10. Drizzle Sauce: Finish by drizzling the southwestern sauce over each corn cake. Serve immediately while hot and enjoy these flavorful, crispy tamale cakes!

This dish is a delicious combination of sweet, spicy, and savory flavors, perfect for vegetarians and non-vegetarians alike!

Shrimp & Avocado Quesadillas with Fresh Pico

Quesadillas are one of the easiest, yet most satisfying dishes to make on the Blackstone. The perfect combination of crunchy, cheesy, spicy, and savory flavors makes them a hit, and they pair beautifully with your favorite dips and salsas. These shrimp quesadillas will quickly become a favorite!

Makes 2 servings

Ingredients:

Pico de Gallo:

- 1 cup (160 g) finely chopped white onion
- 1 jalapeño, ribs and seeds removed, finely chopped
- ¼ cup (60 ml) lime juice
- ¼ teaspoon sea salt, plus more to taste
- 1½ pounds (680 g) ripe red tomatoes, chopped
- ½ cup (8 g) freshly chopped cilantro (about 1 bunch)

Quesadillas:

- 1 pound (454 g) raw shrimp, peeled, deveined, and tails removed
- 1 tablespoon (15 ml) avocado oil
- ½ tablespoon (4 g) Meat Church Holy Voodoo seasoning (or your favorite spicy seasoning)
- 2 large burrito-sized flour tortillas

- 1 large avocado, peeled, halved, and sliced
- 1 cup (113 g) shredded Oaxaca cheese (or your favorite melty cheese)
- Spanish rice, for serving
- Salsa, cilantro lime crema, or guacamole, for serving

Instructions:

1. Make Pico de Gallo: In a large bowl, combine the chopped onion, jalapeño, lime juice, sea salt, tomatoes, and cilantro. Mix well, then refrigerate until ready to use.
2. Prepare the Shrimp: Pat the shrimp dry with paper towels. In a bowl, toss the shrimp with avocado oil and Meat Church Holy Voodoo seasoning, ensuring the shrimp are well-coated.
3. Cook the Shrimp: Heat two burners on your Blackstone griddle to medium-high. Once hot, add the shrimp and cook for 3 to 4 minutes, tossing with a spatula until they curl and are no longer translucent. Remove from heat.
4. Warm the Tortillas: Scrape the griddle clean and lightly oil it again. Place the tortillas on the griddle and warm for about 60 seconds, then flip.
5. Assemble the Quesadillas: In the center of each tortilla, add half of the cooked shrimp, ¼ cup (45 g) of drained pico de gallo, half a sliced avocado, and ½ cup (57 g) of shredded Oaxaca cheese.
6. Fold and Cook: Fold two sides of the tortilla over the center to create an open-ended burrito shape. Carefully flip the quesadillas every minute, cooking for 3 to 4 minutes until the cheese is melted and the tortillas are golden and crispy.
7. Serve: Let the quesadillas rest for a minute, then slice each into quarters. Serve with Spanish rice, additional pico de gallo, and your favorite salsa, guacamole, or cilantro lime crema. Enjoy this flavorful, cheesy treat!

Blackened Mahi Mahi Tacos with Zesty Slaw

Taco Tuesday takes a flavorful turn with these mahi mahi tacos! The mahi mahi fillets have a delicious non-fishy flavor and a hearty texture that pairs perfectly with a crunchy, tangy slaw. These tacos are incredibly easy to make on the Blackstone and will become a new favorite!

Makes 6–12 tacos

Ingredients:

Slaw:

- ◄ 4 ounces (113 g) tricolored coleslaw mix
- ◄ ¼ cup (60 ml) mayonnaise
- ◄ 1 tablespoon (15 ml) apple cider vinegar
- ◄ 2 teaspoons (4 g) Everything But The Bagel seasoning

Tacos:

- ◄ 4 (3–4 oz [84–113 g]) mahi mahi fillets
- ◄ 2 teaspoons (10 ml) avocado oil
- ◄ 4 teaspoons (10 g) Meat Church Holy Voodoo seasoning (or your favorite Cajun seasoning)
- ◄ 6 soft taco-sized flour tortillas or 12 street taco-sized corn tortillas
- ◄ ¼ cup (60 ml) cotija or queso fresco cheese
- ◄ ½ cup (8 g) chopped cilantro
- ◄ Cilantro rice, for serving

Instructions:

1. Start by making the slaw for the tacos. In a bowl, combine the tricolored coleslaw mix, mayonnaise, apple cider vinegar, and Everything But The Bagel seasoning. Mix well and refrigerate while you prepare the tacos.
2. Preheat your griddle to medium-high heat.
3. Pat the mahi mahi fillets dry with paper towels. Lightly coat them with avocado oil and season all sides with Meat Church Holy Voodoo seasoning, using about ½ teaspoon on each side. This helps achieve a nice sear rather than boiling the fish.
4. Place the fillets on the hot griddle and cook the first side for 2 to 3 minutes until the edges start to brown and blacken. Flip the fillets and cook the second side for another 2 to 3 minutes. Once nearly cooked, break them up gently with a spatula. Move the fish to a side burner set to low to keep warm.
5. Reduce the griddle heat to low and add your tortillas. Heat the tortillas for about 30 seconds, then flip them. Distribute the mahi mahi evenly among the tortillas. Top each taco with a generous spoonful of slaw, a sprinkle of cotija cheese, and some chopped cilantro.
6. Serve these tasty tacos with a side of cilantro rice.
7. The combination of spicy blackened mahi mahi and tangy slaw creates a delicious taco experience!

Homemade Crunch Wraps Supreme

Recreating some of my kids' favorite fast-food orders is always a hit in our house. This copycat Taco Bell™ recipe is sure to excite everyone, especially since it's made with quality ingredients and a bit of love. I have a feeling these Crunch Wraps will quickly become a family favorite!

Makes 6 Crunch Wraps

Ingredients:

- 1 pound (454 g) lean ground beef
- 1 medium white onion, chopped
- 2 tablespoons (10 g) taco seasoning
- ¼ cup (60 ml) water
- 1 (15-ounce [425-g]) jar nacho cheese or queso dip
- 6 burrito-sized flour tortillas
- 6 tostada shells (seasoned or unseasoned)
- 1 cup (240 ml) sour cream
- 2 cups (140 g) shredded iceberg lettuce
- 1 large tomato, diced
- 1 cup (113 g) shredded Mexican cheese
- 6 small street taco-sized flour tortillas
- Mexican rice or charro beans, for serving
- Lime wedges, for serving

Instructions:

1. Preheat your lightly oiled griddle to medium-high heat. Cook the ground beef and chopped onion for 6 to 8 minutes until the beef is no longer pink. Drain any excess grease into the rear grease trap. Stir in the taco seasoning and water, mixing well. Continue cooking until the mixture begins to boil. Reduce the heat to medium and let it simmer for 2 to 3 more minutes, stirring occasionally. If there's room on the griddle, push the beef to the side; otherwise, remove it from the heat.
2. In a small pot on the Blackstone, warm the nacho cheese. Meanwhile, warm the flour tortillas on the griddle for about 30 seconds per side. Place the warmed tortillas in a tortilla warmer or between two plates to keep them warm.
3. To assemble the Crunch Wraps, lay one large flour tortilla flat. Spread ½ cup (118 ml) of the seasoned taco meat in the center. Add 2 tablespoons (30 ml) of nacho cheese on top of the meat. Place one tostada shell over the cheese, then spread a thin layer of sour cream on the tostada. Top with shredded lettuce, diced tomato, and shredded Mexican cheese. Be careful not to overfill. Place a small street taco-sized flour tortilla in the center.
4. To fold the Crunch Wrap, start with the bottom edge of the large tortilla and fold it up over the center. Continue folding the tortilla around the filling, working your way around until the center is completely covered.
5. Repeat the assembly process with the remaining tortillas, tostadas, and fillings, yielding a total of 6 Crunch Wraps.
6. Lightly oil your griddle and place as many Crunch Wraps as will fit seam-side down onto the griddle. Cook for 2 to 3 minutes until golden brown. Flip and cook the other side for another 2 to 3 minutes until golden brown as well. Repeat with any remaining Crunch Wraps.
7. Serve with your favorite sides, such as Mexican rice or charro beans, and garnish with lime wedges. Enjoy your delicious homemade Crunch Wraps!

Chapter 3 Blackstone Burgers

Oklahoma Crispy Onion Smash Burgers

When I think of a perfect burger, Oklahoma Smash Burgers are what come to mind! What makes these burgers stand out? It's the unique technique of smashing the onions into the beef while cooking, which infuses incredible flavor. With just a few simple ingredients, you'll find these burgers incredibly easy to prepare. Get ready to impress your friends and family with this backyard classic!

Yields: 4 Burgers

Ingredients:

- 1 large white onion
- 1 pound (454 g) 80/20 ground chuck (2 patties of 2 ounces (56 g) each per burger)
- Pinch of salt and freshly ground black pepper
- 8 slices of American cheese
- Ketchup
- Yellow mustard
- 16 dill pickle slices
- 4 potato roll hamburger buns
- Fries or chips for serving

Instructions:

1. Heat Up Your Griddle: Begin by preheating your lightly oiled Blackstone griddle to high heat. This will create the perfect environment for searing your burgers.
2. Slice the Onion: Thinly slice the onion into paper-thin rings. A mandolin slicer is excellent for achieving the right thickness.
3. Shape the Meat: Form the ground chuck into loose balls, each weighing 2 ounces (56 g). Place these meatballs on the hot griddle. Top each meatball with a portion of the thinly sliced onions—don't worry if some fall off!
4. Smash and Sear: Using a burger smasher, press down firmly on the meatballs and onions to flatten them. To prevent sticking, place a piece of parchment paper between the smasher and the meat. Hold the smasher down for about 10 seconds to ensure a good sear.
5. Season and Cook: Sprinkle a pinch of salt and black pepper (around ¼ teaspoon each) onto the patties. Let them cook for 2 to 3 minutes until you see juices pooling on the surface and the edges begin to brown. This indicates they're ready to flip. If they feel stuck, it's just the crispy layer forming!
6. Add Cheese and Build the Burgers: Once flipped, lower the griddle temperature to low. Allow the residual heat to finish cooking the burgers while adding a slice of American cheese to each patty. Stack the patties two high, then add a swirl of ketchup, yellow mustard, and 4 slices of dill pickles on top.
7. Steam the Buns: Place the top bun on the burger stack and add the bottom bun on top of that. This will allow the buns to steam slightly and warm as the burgers finish cooking.
8. Check for Doneness: After a minute or two, once the cheese is melted, your burgers are ready. Remove the top bun and stack the rest of the ingredients neatly.
9. Serve and Enjoy: Pair your delicious Oklahoma Smash Burgers with your favorite fries or chips for a complete meal. Enjoy the flavors of this backyard favorite!

Green chiles truly elevate any dish, and this burger is no exception! I find myself wanting to whip up this mouthwatering creation every week; it's just that delicious! Don't be intimidated by the green chiles—they bring a gentle heat along with an explosion of flavor.

Makes 4 Burgers

Ingredients:

- ◄ 4 teaspoons (20 ml) mayonnaise, plus extra for topping
- ◄ 4 brioche hamburger buns
- ◄ 1 pound (454 g) 80/20 ground chuck (2 patties of 2 ounces (56 g) each per burger)
- ◄ Pinch of salt and freshly ground black pepper (or your favorite spicy seasoning)
- ◄ 8 slices of pepper Jack cheese
- ◄ 4 ounces (113 g) diced flame-roasted green chiles
- ◄ Fries or chips for serving

Instructions:

1. Begin by preheating your lightly oiled Blackstone griddle to high heat. While it warms up, spread a teaspoon of mayonnaise on each bun and place them cut-side down on the griddle. Toast for 3 to 5 minutes until they're lightly browned, then set them aside.

2. Shape the ground chuck into loose meatballs, each weighing about 2 ounces (56 g). Arrange these meatballs on the hot griddle.

3. Using a burger press, flatten the meatballs. To prevent sticking, you might want to place a piece of parchment paper between the press and the meat. Press down firmly for about 10 seconds; this helps create a nice sear.

4. Season the patties with a pinch of salt and black pepper (around ¼ teaspoon each). For an extra flavor boost, feel free to use your preferred spicy seasoning.

5. Let the patties cook for 2 to 3 minutes. You'll notice juices bubbling up and the edges turning golden brown—this is when you know it's time to flip them. They might feel a bit stuck, but that's just the crispy layer forming!

6. After flipping, reduce the griddle heat to low and let the residual heat finish cooking the patties. Top each one with a slice of pepper Jack cheese. In about 2 minutes, stack the patties two high.

7. While the burgers are nearly finished, add the diced green chiles to the griddle to warm them through. When they start to bubble, place about 1 ounce (28 g) of chiles on top of each burger.

8. Once the cheese has melted, the burgers are ready. Place the stacked patties onto your toasted brioche buns and finish with your favorite condiments, such as more mayonnaise.

9. Serve these delightful burgers alongside your choice of fries or chips for a perfect meal.

Umami Mushroom BBQ Smash Burgers with Furikake

I'm a huge fan of fusion cuisine! There's something magical about combining unexpected ingredients and styles to create a delightful new dish. The umami from shiitake mushrooms pairs beautifully with the sweetness of BBQ sauce, delivering the essence of your favorite Japanese flavors in a gourmet burger format. This particular burger holds a special place in my heart; I won an online food contest with this concept and its photography through Food Beast. Winning that contest opened doors to numerous connections with fellow chefs and content creators, and I'll always be grateful for this amazing smash burger experience! Now it's your turn to explore the deliciousness it brings.

Makes 2 Burgers

Ingredients:

- 4 tablespoons (60 ml) Japanese mayonnaise, divided
- 2 hamburger buns
- 5 ounces (141 g) shiitake mushrooms, cleaned and sliced
- 3 tablespoons (42 g) unsalted butter
- Pinch of salt and freshly ground black pepper, divided
- 4 tablespoons (60 ml) Bachan's Japanese BBQ Sauce (or your favorite teriyaki sauce), divided
- ½ pound (226 g) 80/20 ground chuck (2 patties of 2 ounces (56 g) each per burger)
- 4 slices of white Cheddar cheese
- 2 teaspoons (3 g) Japanese furikake seasoning (a mix of seaweed and sesame seeds)
- 1 bunch green onions, chopped
- Fries, chips, or tater tots for serving

Instructions:

1. Start by setting your lightly oiled griddle to medium-high heat. Spread ½ tablespoon (7 ml) of Japanese mayonnaise on the inside of each hamburger bun. Toast the buns cut-side down on the griddle for 3 to 4 minutes, or until they are golden brown. Remove them from the heat and set aside.

2. While the buns are toasting, melt the butter in a pan and add the sliced shiitake mushrooms. Season them with a pinch of black pepper and 2 tablespoons (30 ml) of Bachan's Japanese BBQ Sauce. Sauté the mushrooms for 3 to 4 minutes until they become soft and slightly browned. Once cooked, move the mushrooms to the side of the griddle or remove them from the heat.

3. Roll the ground chuck into balls, about 2 ounces (56 g) each. Place the meatballs on the hot griddle. Use a burger press to flatten each meatball. To prevent sticking, place a piece of parchment paper between the smasher and the meatball. Apply firm pressure for about 10 seconds to ensure a good sear.

4. Season each patty with a pinch of salt and black pepper, then drizzle about ½ tablespoon (7 ml) of Bachan's BBQ sauce on top. Let them cook until you see juices rising and the edges browning—about 2 to 3 minutes. If they seem stuck, that's just the crispy layer forming. Flip the patties over gently.

5. After flipping, reduce the heat on the griddle to low, allowing residual heat to finish cooking the patties. Top each with a slice of white Cheddar cheese. After about 2 minutes, stack the patties two high. Place the stacked patties onto the toasted buns. Sprinkle Japanese furikake, add a pinch of chopped green onions, and top with the sautéed mushrooms. Drizzle more Japanese mayonnaise on the top bun before placing it on the burger.

6. Snap a few photos for Instagram and enjoy your burger with your favorite fries, chips, or tater tots!

Jalapeño Big Smack Smash Burgers with Tangy Sauce

Smash burgers have become a go-to dish in our home. With just a few simple ingredients, you can create a culinary masterpiece that comes together in no time and impresses even the toughest food critics. The beauty of these burgers lies in their versatility—you can experiment with various ingredients to create your own unique twist. One of my favorite variations features the spicy kick of jalapeños, balanced perfectly by a tangy homemade sauce. Combined with gooey cheese and robust beef flavor, each bite is absolutely incredible.

Makes 4 Burgers

Big Smack Sauce:

- ◀ 1 cup (240 ml) Duke's Mayonnaise
- ◀ ¼ cup (60 ml) ketchup
- ◀ ¼ cup (60 g) sweet relish
- ◀ 1 tablespoon (15 ml) yellow mustard
- ◀ 2 teaspoons (5 g) onion powder
- ◀ 1 teaspoon vinegar

Smash Burgers:

- ◀ 1 medium white onion, thinly sliced
- ◀ 2 large jalapeños, sliced (remove seeds for less heat)
- ◀ 5 teaspoons (12 g) Meat Church Holy Cow seasoning (or your favorite burger seasoning), divided
- ◀ 4 hamburger buns

- ◀ 2 pounds (907 g) 80/20 ground chuck (each burger with 2 ounces (56 g) patties)
- ◀ 12 slices of Colby Jack cheese

Instructions:

1. Begin by preparing the Big Smack Sauce. In a bowl, combine the mayonnaise, ketchup, sweet relish, yellow mustard, onion powder, and vinegar. Mix well and refrigerate until you're ready to use it.

2. In a lightly oiled medium-heat griddle zone, sauté the sliced onion and jalapeños. Season the vegetables with a teaspoon of Meat Church Holy Cow seasoning. Stir the mixture every minute or so. Once the onion becomes translucent, about 4 to 5 minutes, remove it from the heat.

3. While the veggies are cooking, toast the insides of the hamburger buns on the same burners set to medium. This should take about 2 minutes. If using a 36-inch (91-cm) griddle, set the other half to high in preparation for the burger patties. For smaller Blackstone griddles, you may need to complete these steps in batches.

4. For the burger patties, loosely roll the ground chuck into twelve balls, each about 2 ounces (56 g), roughly the size of a racquetball. Place the meatballs on the hot griddle. Allow one side to brown for about 30 seconds before flipping them over. This seared side will help prevent sticking when you smash the patties.

5. Using a flat spatula or burger smasher, flatten each meatball as much as possible, holding down for 10 to 12 seconds. Repeat this for each meatball and season with approximately ¼ teaspoon of the Meat Church Holy Cow seasoning on each smashed patty.

6. Cook the patties for 2 to 3 minutes, watching for juices to rise and the edges to brown. This is your cue to flip them. They might seem stuck, but that's just the crispy layer forming on the smash burger.

7. After flipping, reduce the griddle heat to low and let the residual heat continue cooking the patties. Add a slice of Colby Jack cheese to each patty. Once the cheese melts, in about a minute or two, the patties are done.

8. Assemble your burger on the bottom bun with your desired number of patties—personally, I usually go for three! Top with the sautéed onions, jalapeños, and a generous spoonful of Big Smack Sauce. Finally, crown your creation with the top bun and serve.

Lone Star Smash Melt

Combining two of my favorite burger styles—the smash burger and the patty melt—results in a truly indulgent creation! The key element that elevates this burger is the use of thick Texas toast. With its crunchy exterior and soft, pillowy interior, this burger is sure to impress your family when you whip it up on the Blackstone!

Makes 4 Patty Melts

Ingredients:

- ◄ 8 slices of bacon
- ◄ 8 teaspoons (40 ml) mayonnaise, plus extra for topping
- ◄ 8 slices of thick Texas toast (thick-cut white bread)
- ◄ 1 pound (454 g) 80/20 ground chuck (with 2 patties of 2 ounces (56 g) each per melt)
- ◄ 8 teaspoons (12 g) Blackstone's Whiskey Burger or Pub Burger Seasoning (or your preferred burger seasoning)
- ◄ 1 medium white onion, diced
- ◄ 8 slices of white American cheese
- ◄ Fries, tater tots, or chips for serving

Instructions:

1. Begin by preheating your lightly oiled Blackstone griddle to low heat. Place the bacon slices on the griddle and cook them slowly, flipping every minute to ensure even cooking. This method helps achieve perfectly crispy bacon without burning. After 8 to 10 minutes, remove the bacon when it's almost as crispy as you like; it will continue to crisp as it cools.
2. Once the bacon is cooked, increase the griddle temperature to medium heat.
3. Spread about a teaspoon of mayonnaise on one side of each slice of Texas toast. Place the slices mayo-side down on the griddle until lightly toasted, which should take about 2 to 3 minutes. Keep an eye on them, checking every 30 seconds to prevent burning. Once toasted, remove the slices from the griddle.
4. Turn the griddle heat up to high. Form the ground chuck into loose balls, each weighing about 2 ounces (56 g), roughly the size of a racquetball. Place the meatballs onto the hot griddle.
5. Using a burger press, flatten the meatballs. You might want to put a piece of parchment paper between the press and the meatball to avoid sticking. Press down firmly for about 10 seconds to ensure a nice sear.
6. Season each patty with about a teaspoon of Blackstone's Whiskey Burger seasoning, sprinkling it generously over the top.
7. While the patties cook, add the diced onion to the side of the griddle. The residual heat will sauté the onions beautifully; stir every 30 seconds. Once they're cooked, move them to a corner of the griddle to keep warm.
8. As the patties cook, you'll see juices rising to the surface and the edges browning. After 2 to 3 minutes, gently flip the patties. They may feel stuck, but that's just the crispy exterior forming.
9. After flipping, reduce the griddle heat to low and let the patties continue cooking with residual heat. Top each patty with a slice of white American cheese. In about 2 minutes, when the cheese melts, you can stack the patties two high.
10. Place the double-stacked patties on the untoasted side of one slice of Texas toast. Add a generous amount of sautéed onions, two slices of bacon, and your favorite condiment (I prefer mayonnaise). Top with the final slice of Texas toast and serve alongside fries, tater tots, or chips.

Fiery Chipotle Smash Burgers

Sometimes, you have to push the limits! That's precisely what we did with this enormous, flavorful, and spicy burger. Packed with layer after layer of spicy goodness, it features high-quality chuck brisket and short rib beef patties that create an unforgettable burger experience.

Makes 2 Burgers

Ingredients:

Chipotle Aioli:

- ◀ ¼ cup (60 ml) mayonnaise
- ◀ 1 (7.5-ounce [212-g]) can chipotle peppers in adobo sauce

Burgers:

- ◀ 2 tablespoons (28 g) unsalted butter
- ◀ 2 brioche split-top buns
- ◀ 4 (¼-pound [113-g]) chuck brisket and short rib beef patties (store-bought or substitute any ¼-pound [113-g] beef patties)
- ◀ 4 teaspoons (10 g) Meat Church Holy Voodoo seasoning (or your favorite spicy seasoning)
- ◀ Pinch of ground black pepper
- ◀ 3 large jalapeños (two whole, one sliced)
- ◀ 8 slices of pepper Jack cheese
- ◀ 2 large lettuce leaves
- ◀ ¼ cup (26 g) crispy fried onions

Instructions:

1. Begin by preparing the chipotle aioli for your burgers. Take two chipotle peppers from the can of adobo sauce and mince them finely. In a bowl, mix the minced chipotles with the mayonnaise until well combined. (You can reserve the remaining chipotles for another recipe.)

2. Preheat your lightly oiled griddle to medium-high heat. Add the butter and spread it evenly with a spatula. Toast the brioche buns in the melted butter for about 2 to 3 minutes, or until they turn golden brown. Once toasted, remove them from the heat and set aside.

3. Season the beef patties generously with Meat Church Holy Voodoo seasoning and a pinch of black pepper. Place the patties on the lightly oiled medium-high griddle. Cook for 3 to 4 minutes on each side, or until they reach your preferred level of doneness.

4. While the patties are cooking, add the two whole jalapeños and the sliced jalapeño to the griddle. Flip them every minute to ensure all sides get nicely seared. Once the patties are nearly done, place two slices of pepper Jack cheese on each one. Pour a tablespoon (15 ml) of water onto the griddle and cover the hood to help the cheese melt perfectly.

5. To assemble your burger, start with a large lettuce leaf on the bottom to prevent the bun from getting soggy. Stack two burger patties on top of the lettuce. Finish by adding crispy fried onions, jalapeño slices, and a generous spoonful of the chipotle aioli. For a fun touch, use a bamboo skewer to pierce a seared jalapeño through the top bun to signal the spicy delight inside.

6. Serve your spicy creation with a side of your favorite fries or tater tots for a complete meal!

While we adore smash burgers, sometimes you just crave a hearty burger stacked high with delicious toppings! These thick burgers are perfect for satisfying any BBQ cravings and will make you the star of the next block party with their sweet BBQ sauce and crispy onion rings.

Makes 2 Burgers

Ingredients:

- ◄ 4 frozen onion rings
- ◄ 2 brioche sesame seed hamburger buns
- ◄ 2 teaspoons (10 ml) mayonnaise
- ◄ 2 (5-ounce [141-g]) brisket/chuck burger patties
- ◄ 4 teaspoons (10 g) Meat Church Holy Cow seasoning (or your favorite BBQ rub)
- ◄ 1 small white onion, diced
- ◄ 2 slices of Cheddar cheese
- ◄ 2 lettuce leaves
- ◄ 1 tomato, sliced
- ◄ 2 tablespoons (30 ml) BBQ sauce
- ◄ BBQ-flavored kettle-cooked chips for serving

Instructions:

1. Begin by preheating your lightly oiled Blackstone griddle to medium-high heat.

2. While the griddle warms, place the frozen onion rings in the Blackstone air fryer set to medium. After about 8 minutes, they should come out crispy and golden. If you don't have a Blackstone with an air fryer, you can use a separate air fryer, toaster oven, or conventional oven to cook the onion rings similarly.

3. Spread ½ teaspoon of mayonnaise on the inside of each hamburger bun.

4. Once the griddle reaches the right temperature, toast the buns face down for 2 to 3 minutes, or until they turn golden brown. Remove them from the griddle and set aside.

5. Season each brisket burger patty with 1 teaspoon of Meat Church Holy Cow seasoning on both sides. Place the seasoned patties on the hot griddle, allowing them to sear and brown. Flip the burgers every 2 minutes, cooking until they reach your desired doneness—aim for about 8 to 10 minutes for medium-well.

6. As the burgers cook, add the diced white onion to the griddle. The drippings from the patties will help caramelize the onions beautifully. Stir frequently until the onions become translucent.

7. When the burgers are nearly done, lower the griddle heat to low and let the residual heat finish cooking them. Place a slice of Cheddar cheese on top of each patty. Cover with a lid or dome to facilitate melting.

8. While the cheese is melting, assemble your burgers. Start with a lettuce leaf on the bottom bun, followed by a slice of tomato to keep the bun from getting soggy. Place the cheesy burger patty on top, then add two crispy onion rings. Drizzle a tablespoon (15 ml) of BBQ sauce over the rings and sprinkle half of the sautéed onions on top. Finish with the top bun.

9. Serve these mouthwatering burgers alongside crispy BBQ-flavored kettle-cooked potato chips for the perfect meal.

Chapter 4 weekends supper

Wood-Fired Strip Steak Perfection

The Blackstone is one of my favorite tools to pair with my pellet grills, and the reverse-seared steak is a perfect example of what these two devices can achieve together. The smoky flavor from the Traeger, combined with the exceptional searing power of the Blackstone, creates a steak that rivals anything you'd find in a high-end steakhouse. This technique can be applied to any common cut of beef. If you don't have a pellet grill, you can always sear your steak on the Blackstone and finish it in the oven to reach your desired doneness.

Makes 4 Steaks

Ingredients:

- ◄ 4 (12 ounces [340-g]) New York strip steaks
- ◄ 8 teaspoons (20 g) Meat Church Holy Cow seasoning (or your favorite steak seasoning)
- ◄ 4 tablespoons (57 g) garlic compound butter
- ◄ Loaded baked potatoes or griddled veggies for serving

Instructions:

1. Begin by preheating your pellet grill to the lowest setting, around 165°F (75°C). If your grill has a Super Smoke mode, turn that on as well for added flavor.
2. Generously season each steak with 2 teaspoons (5 g) of Meat Church Holy Cow seasoning on all sides. Place the steaks on the grill, ideally on a rack positioned in the center. Use an internal meat thermometer to monitor the temperature.
3. After about 2½ hours, the steaks should reach approximately 110°F (45°C) internally. At this point, crank the Blackstone up to high heat, ensuring a light layer of oil coats the entire griddle surface. Aim for a surface temperature of around 500°F (260°C).
4. When the steaks hit 110°F (45°C), take them off the grill and place them directly onto the hot Blackstone. Flip the steaks every minute until they reach an internal temperature of 135°F (60°C) for medium rare. This should take just 2 to 3 minutes.
5. Remove the steaks from the griddle and top them with pats of garlic compound butter. Allow the steaks to rest for about 5 minutes to let the juices redistribute before slicing.
6. Serve your delicious steaks alongside loaded baked potatoes or your favorite griddled vegetables for a complete meal.

Tequila Honey Chicken Fajitas Fiesta

Fajitas cooked on the Blackstone are an absolute delight! This recipe, inspired by my friend Matt Pittman, creates some of the most flavorful fajitas you'll ever taste. I knew as soon as I saw it that I had to adapt it for the Blackstone, and it had to make it into this book. Just remember, this dish requires an overnight marinade, so plan ahead—it's well worth the effort!

Makes 4 Servings

Ingredients:

Marinade:

◀ 6 tablespoons (90 ml) olive oil

◀ 6 tablespoons (90 ml) silver tequila

◀ 2 tablespoons (30 ml) hot honey

◀ Zest of 2 limes

◀ Juice of 1 lime

◀ 1 jalapeño, sliced

◀ 4 cloves garlic, grated

◀ 1 tablespoon (7 g) Meat Church Gourmet Garlic and Herb seasoning (or garlic salt)

Fajitas:

◀ 6 boneless, skinless chicken breasts

◀ 1 large white onion, julienned

◀ 1 green bell pepper, julienned

◀ 1 yellow bell pepper, julienned

◀ 1 red bell pepper, julienned

◀ 12 fajita-sized flour tortillas

◀ Spanish rice and black beans for serving

◀ Salsa for serving

Instructions:

1. In a bowl, combine the olive oil, silver tequila, hot honey, lime zest, lime juice, sliced jalapeño, grated garlic, and Meat Church Gourmet Garlic and Herb seasoning. Mix well. Add the chicken breasts to the marinade, ensuring they are well coated. Cover and refrigerate overnight to let the flavors meld.

2. The next day, preheat one side of your lightly oiled Blackstone griddle to medium heat. Remove the chicken from the marinade and place it directly on the griddle along with the julienned onion and bell peppers.

3. Allow the chicken to cook for 3 to 4 minutes before flipping it. Cook the other side for an additional 3 to 4 minutes, then continue flipping the chicken every minute until it reaches an internal temperature of 165°F (75°C), which should take about 8 to 10 minutes total. Once cooked, remove the chicken from the griddle and let it rest for 5 to 10 minutes.

4. Cook the veggies on the griddle until they soften and take on some color, about 5 to 6 minutes, then remove them from the heat.

5. While the chicken is resting, warm the flour tortillas on the griddle for 2 to 3 minutes on each side.

6. Slice the rested chicken and serve it on the warm tortillas, topped with a generous portion of sautéed veggies.

7. Pair these delicious fajitas with Spanish rice, black beans, and your favorite salsa for a complete meal!

Rib Eye Crostini with Horseradish Cream

I often host large groups from our church, so I'm always on the lookout for recipes that can feed a crowd. This crostini recipe features tender, juicy rib eye steak strips and a satisfying crunch from the baguette, making it an excellent appetizer or a delightful addition to a multi-course meal.

Makes 20 Crostini

Ingredients:

- ◀ 1 boneless rib eye steak, ½″ to 1″ (1.3 to 2.5 cm) thick
- ◀ Horseradish Sauce:
- ◀ 1 cup (240 ml) sour cream
- ◀ 2 tablespoons (30 ml) mayonnaise
- ◀ 4 tablespoons (60 ml) prepared horseradish
- ◀ 2 tablespoons (6 g) finely chopped chives
- ◀ 2 teaspoons (10 ml) Dijon mustard
- ◀ Pinch of salt and freshly ground black pepper

Crostini:

- ◀ 1 baguette, sliced into ½″ (1.3-cm)-thick slices (approximately 20 slices)
- ◀ ¼ cup (60 ml) extra virgin olive oil
- ◀ Pinch of salt and freshly ground black pepper
- ◀ Balsamic glaze for drizzling
- ◀ 2 tablespoons (6 g) chopped chives for garnish

Instructions:

1. Begin by letting the rib eye steak come to room temperature while you prepare the horseradish sauce and crostini. In a bowl, combine the sour cream, mayonnaise, horseradish, chopped chives, Dijon mustard, salt, and black pepper. Whisk until smooth, then refrigerate until you're ready to use it.

2. Preheat your lightly oiled griddle to medium-high heat. Brush each slice of baguette with olive oil. Place the baguette slices on the griddle and toast for 2 to 4 minutes per side, or until they are lightly golden brown. Once done, remove them from the heat.

3. Increase the griddle temperature to high heat. Pat the rib eye steak dry with paper towels and season both sides with a pinch of salt and black pepper.

4. Add a tablespoon (15 ml) of olive oil to the hot griddle. Place the steak on the griddle and use a burger press to ensure it makes good contact with the cooking surface. Cook for 2 minutes, then flip the steak and cook for another 2 minutes. Repeat this process for a total cooking time of 8 minutes.

5. Transfer the steak to a cutting board and loosely cover it with foil. Allow it to rest for 5 minutes. After resting, slice the steak thinly, aiming for at least 20 slices to top each baguette slice.

6. Assemble the crostini by placing a slice of steak on each baguette piece. Top with a dollop of horseradish sauce, a drizzle of balsamic glaze, and a sprinkle of chopped chives. Arrange them on a platter and enjoy as they quickly disappear!

Mayo-Marinated Juicy Chicken Breasts

Mayo-marinated chicken might sound surprising, but trust me—it's a game changer! I had my doubts when I first heard about it, but after trying it thanks to Blackstone Betty, I'm now a fan. This simple process results in some of the juiciest and most flavorful chicken you'll ever make on the griddle!

Makes 4 Servings

Ingredients:

- ½ cup (120 ml) Duke's Mayonnaise (or any non-vegan mayonnaise)
- 1 tablespoon (5 g) Blackstone's Whiskey Burger seasoning (or your preferred all-purpose seasoning)
- 4 boneless, skinless chicken breasts

Instructions:

1. In a bowl, combine the mayonnaise and seasoning, mixing until well blended.
2. Place the chicken breasts in a large zip-top bag and pour the seasoned mayonnaise over them. Seal the bag and mix gently to ensure the chicken is fully coated. Let it marinate in the refrigerator for at least 20 minutes, or up to 4 hours for more flavor.
3. When you're ready to cook, preheat your griddle to medium-low. Since the mayonnaise contains oil, there's no need to add any extra oil to the griddle. Lay the marinated chicken on the hot surface and cook for 4 to 5 minutes on each side, or until golden brown. The chicken is done when its internal temperature reaches 165°F (75°C) at the thickest part of the breast.
4. After cooking, let the chicken rest for 2 to 3 minutes before slicing. Enjoy it in your favorite salad, wraps, or served alongside griddled veggies for a delicious meal!

Southern Comfort Chicken Fried Steak with Bacon Gravy

Growing up in Texas, I always assumed chicken fried steak was a staple in every American home. It wasn't until I met my wife in high school that I realized not everyone had experienced the deliciousness of this crispy steak dish. Let's change that! I can't wait for you to enjoy this amazing Southern classic, no matter where you are reading this book.

Makes 4 Steaks

Ingredients:

Chicken Fried Steaks:

- 1 pound (454 g) pre-tenderized cube steaks or round steaks (about 4 steaks)
- 2 teaspoons (12 g) salt, plus more to taste
- 3 large eggs, beaten
- 1 cup (240 ml) buttermilk
- 2 cups (250 g) all-purpose flour
- 1½ teaspoons (7 g) garlic powder
- 1 teaspoon coarse ground black pepper
- ½ teaspoon cayenne pepper
- 1 teaspoon Blackstone Breakfast Blend seasoning
- 1 cup (240 ml) canola oil

Bacon Gravy:

- 3 tablespoons (45 ml) reserved cooking oil (or bacon grease, if available)
- 3 tablespoons (24 g) all-purpose flour
- 2 cups (480 ml) heavy cream, plus more as needed

For Serving:

- 2 pounds (907 g) Bob Evans Mashed Potatoes, prepared according to package directions

- 4 slices cooked bacon, crumbled
- Kosher salt to taste
- 1 teaspoon Blackstone Breakfast Blend seasoning
- Freshly ground black pepper to taste

- Chopped parsley for garnish

Instructions:

1. Ensure your steaks are evenly tenderized. If necessary, place plastic wrap over them and use a meat tenderizing mallet to pound them to your desired thickness. Lightly sprinkle the steaks with salt.
2. In a large, shallow bowl, combine the beaten eggs and buttermilk to create the wash.
3. In another large, shallow bowl, mix together the flour, salt, garlic powder, black pepper, cayenne, and Blackstone Breakfast Blend seasoning until well combined. This will be your dredging mixture.
4. Preheat your griddle by turning on the middle two burners to medium heat. Pour the canola oil onto the griddle.
5. While the oil heats up, dredge each steak in the flour mixture, making sure all sides are coated. Then dip it into the egg wash, ensuring it's fully covered before returning it to the dredging mixture. Press the steak into the flour again for a thick coating, and do not shake off any excess. Repeat this process for all steaks.
6. Once the oil is hot enough, test it by dropping a small bit of flour into the oil. If it sizzles and fries immediately, you're ready to cook. Carefully place each coated steak into the oil for shallow frying. Let them cook undisturbed until the edges turn golden brown, about 3 to 4 minutes. Flip the steaks and cook for another 3 to 4 minutes until they are golden and crispy. Transfer the fried steaks to a warming rack off to the side to keep warm.
7. Reserve 3 tablespoons (45 ml) of the cooking oil, then scrape and clean the griddle. If necessary, add a thin layer of fresh oil to maintain the griddle's seasoning.
8. Place a pot on the griddle over medium heat. Add the reserved cooking oil and 3 tablespoons (24 g) of flour to the pot. Whisk continuously and cook until the mixture turns the color of light chocolate milk, about 4 to 5 minutes. Gradually pour in the heavy cream, stirring constantly. Add the crumbled bacon to the mixture. If the gravy is too thick, thin it out by adding heavy cream, one tablespoon (15 ml) at a time, until you reach your desired consistency. Season with salt, Blackstone Breakfast Blend seasoning, and plenty of black pepper to taste.
9. Serve the fried steaks alongside the prepared mashed potatoes, generously smothered in bacon gravy. Garnish with chopped parsley and enjoy hot!

Blackened Salmon with Cajun Crawfish Cream Sauce and Dirty Rice

I absolutely love crawfish! Whether they're fried, boiled, or grilled, I enjoy them in every way possible. As I expanded my culinary skills, I knew I had to incorporate crawfish into as many recipes as I could. In this dish, the creamy and rich sauce complements the blackened Cajun-seasoned salmon perfectly. Plus, the dirty rice is there to soak up any sauce that drips to the bottom of your plate. I promise you're going to adore this meal!

Makes 4 Servings

Ingredients:
Dirty Rice:
- 8 ounces (226 g) boxed dirty rice mix
- 1 (14-ounce [392-g]) can fire-roasted diced tomatoes, drained

Cajun Crawfish Sauce:
- 2 tablespoons (30 ml) olive oil, divided
- 3 tablespoons (42 g) minced shallots (reserve tablespoon (14 g) for garnish)
- ½ cup (80 g) diced yellow onion
- 1 tablespoon (8 g) minced garlic
- 1 pound (454 g) crawfish tails, cooked and peeled
- 2 teaspoons (5 g) Meat Church Holy Voodoo seasoning (or your favorite Cajun seasoning)
- 1 tablespoon (14 g) unsalted butter
- 2 cups (480 ml) heavy cream
- 1 tablespoon (15 ml) jalapeño hot sauce
- 1 tablespoon (15 ml) Worcestershire sauce
- Salt and ground black pepper, to taste

Salmon:
- 4 (5-ounce [141-g]) skinless salmon fillets
- 4 teaspoons (20 ml) avocado oil
- 4 teaspoons (10 g) Meat Church Holy Voodoo seasoning (or your favorite Cajun seasoning)
- ¼ cup (12 g) chopped green onions for garnish

Instructions:

1. Begin by preparing the dirty rice according to the package instructions. You can do this on the Blackstone or a side burner. Before cooking, mix in the fire-roasted diced tomatoes, leaving out any optional added protein.

2. Now for the sauce! In a lightly oiled griddle set to medium heat, add 1 tablespoon (15 ml) of olive oil. Once heated, sauté the shallots and diced onion for 2 to 3 minutes until they become tender. Add the minced garlic and cook for an additional 30 seconds until fragrant. Stir in the crawfish and season with Meat Church Holy Voodoo seasoning. Cook for another 2 to 3 minutes, letting the crawfish brown slightly. Reserve a few crawfish for garnish.

3. In a pot on the griddle set to medium-high heat, combine the remaining tablespoon (15 ml) of olive oil, the sautéed crawfish and vegetables, and the butter. Once the butter begins to melt, slowly pour in the heavy cream while stirring constantly. Add the hot sauce and Worcestershire sauce. Bring the mixture to a low boil, then reduce the heat to a low simmer. Stir frequently for 8 to 12 minutes, until the sauce thickens. Season with salt and black pepper to taste.

4. While the sauce is simmering, prepare the salmon. Pat the salmon fillets dry with paper towels. Drizzle each fillet with 1 teaspoon of avocado oil and generously coat with Meat Church Holy Voodoo seasoning. Place the salmon on a lightly oiled griddle and cook for approximately 5 minutes per side, or until fully cooked through. The seasoning contains a bit of sugar, which will create a nice blackened crust.

5. To serve, plate the dirty rice topped with the blackened salmon and drizzle with the crawfish sauce. Garnish with the reserved green onions, remaining minced shallots, and the reserved sautéed crawfish. This dish is a fantastic Cajun meal that I know you will love!

Garlic Butter Seared Scallops with Fresh Basil

Put on your fancy pants and get ready to create a dish worthy of royalty! Scallops always seemed intimidating to me, but once I tried cooking them on the Blackstone, I found they were surprisingly easy and incredibly flavorful. Whether as an appetizer, side dish, or main course, this recipe is sure to impress your friends at the next block party!

Makes 4 Servings

Ingredients:

- ◀ 1½ pounds (680 g) large sea scallops
- ◀ Pinch of salt and freshly ground black pepper
- ◀ 2 tablespoons (30 ml) olive oil (or a high-heat oil)
- ◀ 2 tablespoons (28 g) unsalted butter
- ◀ 2 cloves garlic, minced
- ◀ ½ cup (12 g) fresh basil leaves, roughly chopped, for garnish
- ◀ 4 lemon slices for serving

Instructions:

1. Begin by patting the scallops dry with a paper towel. This step is crucial for achieving a nice sear. Season one side of each scallop with a pinch of salt and black pepper.
2. Preheat your lightly oiled griddle to medium-high heat and add the olive oil. Once the oil is hot, carefully place the scallops seasoned side down on the griddle. Cook them undisturbed for about 2 minutes until the bottoms are golden brown.
3. Season the unseasoned side of the scallops with a pinch of salt and black pepper. Gently flip the scallops; if they stick, give them a little wiggle to help release them.
4. As soon as you flip the scallops, add the butter and minced garlic to the griddle. Use a food-safe silicone brush to baste the scallops with the melted butter and garlic while they continue to cook for another minute or two. Both sides should be nicely browned.
5. Remove the scallops and garlic from the griddle. Top the scallops with the chopped basil and arrange the lemon slices on the side. These scallops pair wonderfully with an orzo rice pilaf for a complete meal.

Cajun Shrimp and Grits with Spicy Hot Links

There's no meal I crave quite like shrimp and grits! The creamy, buttery, cheesy grits paired with flavorful shrimp are a match made in heaven. To elevate this dish even further, I decided to add some hot link sausages, and it turned out to be a fantastic decision. Unlike traditional outdoor grilling, where natural juices can be lost, cooking on a Blackstone allows all those delicious flavors to stay in the dish, enhancing the shrimp and sausage experience.

Makes 2 Servings

Ingredients:

- 2 cups (480 ml) milk
- 2 cups (480 ml) water
- 1 teaspoon salt
- 1 cup (167 g) yellow corn polenta grits
- ½ pound (226 g) hot link sausages, sliced
- ½ pound (226 g) shrimp, deveined and peeled
- 2 teaspoons (5 g) Meat Church Holy Voodoo seasoning (or your favorite Cajun seasoning)
- 2 tablespoons (28 g) unsalted butter
- 1 bunch fresh chives, chopped, for garnish
- ¼ cup (25 g) grated Parmesan cheese, for garnish
- Hot sauce, to taste

Instructions:

1. Start by preparing the grits. In a medium pot on the griddle set to high heat, bring the milk, water, and salt to a boil. Gradually whisk in the polenta grits and then reduce the heat to low. Allow the grits to simmer slowly for about 30 minutes, stirring occasionally. Once done, remove from heat, cover, and let them sit for 1 to 2 minutes.

2. With about 10 minutes left for the grits, turn on another burner to medium-high heat. Add the sliced hot link sausages to the griddle and cook for approximately 3 minutes, turning until both sides are nicely browned.

3. Next, add the shrimp to the sausages on the griddle. Stir to combine; the shrimp will cook in the sausage drippings, so no additional oil is necessary. Sprinkle the Meat Church Holy Voodoo seasoning over the mixture and cook until the shrimp turn from translucent to opaque, about 2 to 3 minutes. Then, remove from heat.

4. To serve, place a portion of the creamy grits in each bowl and add a tablespoon (14 g) of butter on top. Spoon the shrimp and sausage mixture over the grits. Garnish with chopped chives, grated Parmesan, and a drizzle of hot sauce for an extra kick.

Surf 'n' Turf Rib Eye with Smashed Potatoes and Herbed Butter

Get ready to put your fancy pants on and prepare a meal fit for royalty! This surf and turf dish combines tender rib eye steaks with creamy smashed potatoes and buttery shrimp, all cooked to perfection on the griddle. Cooking on the Blackstone not only enhances the flavors but also keeps everything juicy. Let's dive into this delightful recipe!

Makes 2 Servings

Ingredients:
Turf:
- ◂ 2 rib eye steaks
- ◂ 2 tablespoons (10 g) Blackstone's Steakhouse Seasoning Blend (or your favorite steak seasoning)
- ◂ 1 tablespoon (15 ml) olive oil

Smashed Potatoes:
- ◂ 1 pound (454 g) petite medley potatoes
- ◂ 2 tablespoons (30 ml) olive oil
- ◂ Blackstone's Steakhouse Seasoning Blend (or your favorite steak seasoning), to taste

Herbed Garlic Butter:
- ◂ 1 stick (114 g) unsalted butter
- ◂ 1 tablespoon (2 g) chopped fresh rosemary
- ◂ 1 tablespoon (4 g) chopped parsley

Surf:
- ◂ 1 bunch broccolini, washed and trimmed
- ◂ Pinch of salt and freshly ground black pepper
- ◂ 1 pound (454 g) shrimp, deveined, peeled, and tails removed

- ◂ ¼ cup (12 g) chopped green onion
- ◂ 1 tablespoon (8 g) garlic paste
- ◂ Pinch of salt and freshly ground black pepper

- ◂ 1 tablespoon (15 ml) olive oil
- ◂ Blackstone's Steakhouse Seasoning Blend (or your favorite steak seasoning), to taste

Instructions:

1. Start by allowing the rib eye steaks to come to room temperature. Once they have, pat them dry with a paper towel. Season all sides with the Blackstone Steakhouse Seasoning Blend and let them sit while you prepare the other ingredients.
2. Boil the petite medley potatoes in a large pot of salted water for about 15 minutes until fork-tender. You can do this on the Blackstone set to high heat or on a side burner. Once cooked, remove the potatoes from the water and set them aside.
3. Preheat one side of your griddle to medium-high heat and add 2 tablespoons (30 ml) of olive oil.
4. In a small cast iron skillet or pot placed on the griddle, combine the butter, rosemary, parsley, green onion, garlic paste, salt, and black pepper. Heat over low heat for 6 to 7 minutes, stirring until the butter melts and the herbs become fragrant.
5. Add the boiled potatoes to the medium-high heat side of the griddle. Season them with a few shakes of the Blackstone Steakhouse Seasoning Blend and drizzle a couple of tablespoons (28 g) of the herbed butter over them. Using a spatula or burger smasher, flatten the potatoes until they're nice and flat. Cook until the edges start to brown, about 5 to 6 minutes.
6. While the potatoes are cooking, add the broccolini to the griddle. Season with a pinch of salt and black pepper and cook for about 4 to 5 minutes, until softened and lightly seared. Spoon some of the herbed butter over the broccolini just before removing.
7. Once the potatoes and broccolini are done, move them to the low or off side of the griddle to keep warm. Scrape the griddle and add a light layer of oil for the steaks, about 1 tablespoon (15 ml).
8. Increase the griddle temperature to high. When the oil starts to shimmer and emit small wisps of white smoke, add the rib eye steaks to the griddle. Sear for approximately 2 minutes, then flip and sear for another 2 minutes. Continue to flip every 60 seconds until the steaks reach your desired doneness, about 5 to 6 minutes for medium rare (internal temperature of 130°F (55°C)).
9. After cooking, allow the steaks to rest for 5 minutes. Reduce the griddle heat to medium-high and scrape it clean, adding another light layer of oil if needed.
10. Pat the shrimp dry with paper towels. Drizzle them with 1 tablespoon (15 ml) of oil and toss to coat lightly. Season with a few shakes of the Steakhouse Seasoning Blend and mix well. Add the shrimp to the medium-high heat side of the griddle, stirring frequently until they turn opaque and start to brown, about 2 to 3 minutes.
11. To serve, divide the smashed potatoes, broccolini, and shrimp between two plates. Slice the rib eye steaks and arrange them on top of the potatoes. Drizzle any remaining herbed butter over the steak.
12. Sit back and enjoy this incredible Surf 'n' Turf meal prepared on the Blackstone!

Chapter 5 Pizzas, Breads, and Sandwiches

Griddled Muffuletta Magic: A New Orleans Classic

Few sandwiches can make my mouth water like a classic New Orleans-style muffuletta! The combination of savory olive tapenade, warm deli meats, and melted cheese creates a flavor explosion, especially when griddled to perfection on the Blackstone. While a traditional muffuletta uses a special "muff" bun that can be hard to find, an Italian sourdough round makes an excellent substitute.

Makes 4 Sandwich Quarters

Ingredients:

- 1 Italian sourdough round loaf
- 2 tablespoons (30 ml) mayonnaise
- 2 ounces (56 g) thinly sliced turkey breast
- 2 ounces (56 g) thinly sliced smoked ham
- 6 slices provolone cheese
- ½ cup (120 ml) water
- 1 cup (60 g) olive tapenade

Instructions:

1. Preheat your lightly oiled griddle to medium heat. Carefully slice the Italian sourdough round loaf in half horizontally. Spread mayonnaise on the cut sides of both the top and bottom buns. Place the mayo-coated sides down on the griddle and toast for about 5 minutes, checking every minute to prevent burning.

2. While the bun is toasting, add the turkey and ham to the griddle to warm and lightly brown them.

3. Once the bun is toasted, transfer the bottom half to a warming rack over the griddle. Layer the warmed turkey and ham onto the bottom bun. Evenly distribute the provolone cheese on top. Pour the water onto the griddle and cover with the hood or dome to help the cheese melt. After about 5 minutes, the cheese should be perfectly melted. Top the melted cheese with the olive tapenade, then place the top bun on.

4. Carefully remove the sandwich from the heat and slice it into your desired portions. I recommend cutting it into quarters to share with the whole family!

Nashville Heatwave Hot Chicken Sandwich with Pimento Cheese

I'm absolutely obsessed with Nashville Hot flavors, and I'm not shy about it! This spicy, crispy, and utterly delicious sandwich is a flavor explosion. The addition of creamy pimento cheese perfectly balances the heat. Get ready to take your taste buds on a wild ride!

Makes 4 Sandwiches

Ingredients:

Fried Chicken:

- 10 ounces (283 g) all-purpose flour
- 2 tablespoons (14 g) Meat Church Holy Voodoo seasoning (or your favorite Cajun seasoning)
- 2 large eggs
- 1 cup (240 ml) buttermilk
- 1 tablespoon (15 ml) hot sauce
- 4 boneless, skinless chicken thighs

Spicy Coating:

- ½ cup (120 ml) hot frying oil (from frying the chicken)
- 2 tablespoons (11 g) cayenne pepper (adjust to taste)
- 1 tablespoon (14 g) brown sugar
- 1 tablespoon (7 g) Meat Church Holy Voodoo seasoning (or your favorite Cajun seasoning)

Assembling:

- 4 hamburger buns
- 16 dill pickle slices
- 4 ounces (113 g) pimento cheese
- 4 teaspoons (20 ml) mayonnaise
- Tater tot medallions for serving

Instructions:

1. In a large cast-iron skillet, pour vegetable oil until it's half full. Place the skillet on your well-oiled griddle over high heat and heat the oil to 325°F (165°C).
2. For the dry dredge, mix the flour and Meat Church Holy Voodoo seasoning in a large shallow bowl. In another bowl, whisk together the eggs, buttermilk, and hot sauce.
3. Begin by dipping each chicken thigh into the flour mixture, coating all sides thoroughly. Next, dip the chicken into the egg mixture, ensuring it's well coated. Finish with another dip in the flour mixture and then carefully place the chicken into the hot oil. Fry for 8 to 10 minutes, or until golden brown and the internal temperature reaches 165°F (75°C). Repeat for each thigh.
4. To prepare the spicy coating, mix the reserved hot oil with cayenne pepper, brown sugar, and Meat Church Holy Voodoo seasoning in a separate bowl. Spoon this spicy mixture over the fried chicken to your desired heat level.
5. Assemble each sandwich by placing 4 dill pickle slices on the bottom half of each hamburger bun. Add a fried chicken thigh, followed by 1 ounce (28 g) of pimento cheese and a teaspoon of mayonnaise.
6. Serve these delightful sandwiches with crispy tater tot medallions, cooked in the Blackstone air fryer for an extra crunch!

Cheesy Steak Smash Delight: A Griddled Masterpiece

Let's be clear: I'm not even going to call this a "Philly" cheesesteak. The debate over what defines a true cheesesteak is as heated as the beans vs. no beans in chili argument! Regardless of the name, this hot, cheesy, and incredibly easy sandwich is a must-have on the Blackstone!

Makes 3 Cheesesteaks

Ingredients:

- 14 ounces (392 g) shaved beef steak
- 4 teaspoons (6 g) Blackstone Essential Blend seasoning, divided (or any all-purpose seasoning with salt, pepper, and garlic)
- 1 medium white onion, sliced
- 9 slices white American cheese
- 3 Martin's Hoagie Rolls (I know, I know—I'm already breaking the rules)
- Jalapeño kettle-cooked chips for serving

Instructions:

1. Preheat your Blackstone to medium-high heat, applying a light layer of oil. Once you see small wisps of white smoke rising, you're ready to start cooking.
2. Add the shaved beef to the hot griddle. As it sizzles, use two spatulas to break it apart and chop it into bite-sized pieces. The tough surface of the griddle can handle it! After chopping, let the meat sizzle for 30 seconds to a minute before tossing. Season with 3 teaspoons (5 g) of the Blackstone Essential Blend (or your favorite SPG seasoning) and mix well.
3. While the steak is cooking, add the sliced onion to another medium-high burner on the griddle. Stir the onions every minute, adding a teaspoon of the Blackstone Essential Blend for flavor.
4. After about 5 minutes, combine the steak and onions on the griddle. Let them cook together for another 4 to 5 minutes, allowing both the steak and onions to develop a nice sear.
5. Once seared, divide the steak and onion mixture into three piles that roughly match the size of your hoagie rolls. Top each pile with three slices of white American cheese. Trust me, you're going to love what's coming next!
6. After adding the cheese, pour a couple of teaspoons (10 ml) of water onto the griddle a few inches away from the cheese and steak. Close the hood or dome to create steam, which will help the cheese melt.
7. After a minute, lift the lid and check your cheesy masterpiece. If the cheese hasn't fully melted, let it go for another minute.
8. Once the cheese is perfectly melted, open your hoagie rolls and place them face down on top of each cheesy pile. Close the lid again and allow the buns to steam for 1 to 2 minutes.
9. After steaming, carefully slide a spatula under each pile, supporting the top of the bun with your hand. Flip it over to reveal a gloriously messy creation of steak and cheese goodness. Plate your cheesesteak and repeat the process for the other two sandwiches.
10. Serve these delicious sandwiches with jalapeño kettle chips or whatever sides you love.
11. Congratulations—you've just made an incredible cheesesteak!

Cheddar Bay Chicken Bliss: The Ultimate Griddle Stack

When I got my hands on these Cheddar Bay buns from Signature Baking, I immediately envisioned this sandwich. Inspired by Blackstone Betty's creative recipes and mayo-marinated chicken dishes, this creation is a delicious tribute to great flavors. We whipped these up on our 22-inch (56-cm) Adventure Ready Blackstone during a trip to Clayton, Oklahoma, where the views were stunning—but just wait until you see this sandwich!

Makes 4 Sandwiches

Ingredients:

- 4 chicken breast cutlets, pounded to ¼″ (6-mm) thickness
- 3 cups (720 ml) pickle juice
- 3 tablespoons (45 ml) Chick-fil-A® sauce, plus extra for garnish
- 4 Cheddar buns
- 2 tablespoons (28 g) unsalted butter
- 8 slices thick-cut bacon
- 8 ounces (226 g) sliced baby portabella mushrooms
- Pinch of salt and freshly ground black pepper
- 8 teaspoons (20 g) Meat Church The Gospel seasoning, divided (or your favorite all-purpose seasoning)
- 4 slices Colby Jack cheese
- 1 tablespoon (3 g) diced chives
- 4 lettuce leaves
- 1 tomato, sliced
- 8 pickle slices

Instructions:

1. Begin by marinating the chicken breast cutlets in pickle juice for about 2 hours. After marinating, thoroughly dry the chicken and place it in a bowl with the Chick-fil-A sauce, ensuring each piece is well-coated. Let the chicken soak in the sauce while you prepare the other ingredients.
2. Preheat your lightly oiled griddle to medium heat. Brush each side of the Cheddar buns with ½ tablespoon (7 g) of butter and toast them on the griddle. After approximately 5 minutes, the buns should be nicely toasted. Remove them from the heat.
3. Place the bacon on the griddle, flipping it every minute or so until it reaches your desired crispiness, about 6 to 8 minutes. While the bacon cooks, add the sliced mushrooms to the griddle, seasoning them with salt and black pepper. Once cooked, remove both the bacon and mushrooms from the griddle. Use a scraper to transfer most of the leftover bacon grease to the rear grease trap.
4. Take the chicken cutlets from the marinade, shaking off any excess. Season both sides with 1 teaspoon of Meat Church The Gospel seasoning, then place them on the griddle. Flip the cutlets every 2 minutes until they reach an internal temperature of 165°F (75°C), which should take about 8 to 10 minutes total.
5. When the chicken is nearly done, top each cutlet with mushrooms, bacon, and a slice of Colby Jack cheese. Cover with the hood or dome for 1 to 2 minutes to melt the cheese. Once melted, sprinkle the chives on top and add another shake of Meat Church The Gospel seasoning.
6. Assemble the sandwiches on the toasted Cheddar buns. Layer each with lettuce, a slice of tomato, two pickle slices, and a generous drizzle of Chick-fil-A sauce. The combination of the seasoning and the sauce will create a delightful burst of flavor and color!

Fiesta Grilled Chicken Sandwich with Pico de Gallo Punch

I came across an ad for the Pico de Gallo Chicken Sandwich from Whataburger™ not too long ago, and it caught my eye with its grilled chicken, pico de gallo, pepper Jack cheese, and cilantro lime sauce. I thought, "I can recreate that!" And let me tell you, I'm so glad I did! This sandwich turned out incredible, especially when cooked on the Blackstone.

Makes 2 Sandwiches

Ingredients:

- 2 boneless, skinless chicken breasts
- 2 teaspoons (4 g) fajita seasoning
- 2 teaspoons (10 ml) mayonnaise
- 2 seeded brioche hamburger buns
- 2 slices pepper Jack cheese
- ½ cup (90 g) pico de gallo
- 2 teaspoons (10 ml) cilantro lime crema

Instructions:

1. Begin by pounding the chicken breasts until they are about ¼ inch (6 mm) thick. Season both sides of each breast with 1 teaspoon of fajita seasoning. Heat a light drizzle of avocado oil on a medium-heat griddle and cook the chicken, flipping occasionally, until it reaches an internal temperature of 165°F (75°C), which should take about 8 to 10 minutes

2. While the chicken cooks, spread 1 teaspoon of mayonnaise on each seeded brioche bun. Place the buns on the griddle and toast them until golden and crispy, approximately 4 minutes.

3. Once the buns are toasted, place a slice of pepper Jack cheese on each bottom bun. Cover with a dome to help the cheese melt. After the cheese has melted, layer the grilled chicken on top, followed by ¼ cup (45 g) of pico de gallo. Drizzle with cilantro lime crema before adding the top bun.

4. These sandwiches turned out absolutely amazing—way better than the ad I initially saw! Give this recipe a try; you won't regret it!

Texas Brisket Bomb BBQ Sandwiches

As a Texan, I have a deep appreciation for brisket. Whether you smoke your own or grab some from your favorite local BBQ joint, brisket is a protein that truly shines when warmed up on the griddle. As it heats, the fat renders into delicious beef tallow, allowing the brisket to cook in its own juices, creating an explosion of flavor. These chopped brisket sandwiches offer a quick and easy way to savor the rich, low-and-slow flavor reminiscent of your favorite Texas BBQ spot right off the Blackstone Griddle.

Makes 4 Sandwiches

Ingredients:

- 4 cups (880 g) smoked chopped brisket
- 4 potato roll hamburger buns
- 8 teaspoons (40 ml) mayonnaise
- ½ cup (120 ml) Sweet Baby Ray's BBQ sauce (or your favorite BBQ sauce)
- 16–24 dill pickle slices
- 1 small white onion, sliced
- Tater tots for serving

Instructions:

1. Begin by preheating your lightly oiled griddle with all burners set to medium-low heat (see Tip).

2. On one side of the griddle, add the chopped brisket. If your brisket isn't already chopped, use a spatula to break it apart while it cooks. The sturdy griddle can handle it! Stir continuously as the brisket warms up.

3. Spread about 1 teaspoon of mayonnaise on the inside of each bun, both top and bottom. Place the mayo side down on the griddle to toast. After 3 to 5 minutes, the buns should be golden brown. Keep an eye on them, checking every minute. Once toasted, remove the buns from the heat and set them aside.

4. Once the brisket is warmed through (about 8 to 10 minutes), add the Sweet Baby Ray's BBQ sauce and mix well on the griddle. Keep the heat at medium-low to prevent the sugars in the sauce from burning. Allow the mixture to warm and thicken for 1 to 2 minutes, then turn off all burners.

5. To assemble, place 1 cup (220 g) of the BBQ brisket on each bottom bun. Top with 4 to 6 dill pickle slices and a few slices of white onion, classic additions for Texas BBQ. Finish with the top bun.

6. We paired these Chopped Brisket Sandwiches with crispy tater tots cooked in the Blackstone Air Fryer for about 15 minutes (remember to give them a shake every 3 minutes).

7. TIP: Don't hesitate to slow down your cooking by lowering the temperature a bit. You'll find that a slower pace leads to a more enjoyable cooking experience and better results.

Zesty Griddled Steak Gyros with Fresh Veggie Crunch

This quick marinated steak gyro bursts with incredible flavors and textures, all coming together beautifully on the Blackstone. As the steak sears on the griddle, its juices meld with the marinade to create a delicious crust. The fresh veggies add a refreshing crunch, making this gyro absolutely unforgettable.

Makes 4 Gyros

Ingredients:

Marinade:

- ⅓ cup (80 ml) extra virgin olive oil
- Juice of ½ lemon
- 3 cloves garlic, minced
- 1 teaspoon dried oregano
- ½ teaspoon paprika
- 1 teaspoon salt
- Pinch of freshly ground black pepper
- ½ cup (120 ml) 2% plain Greek yogurt
- 2 tablespoons (30 ml) water

Gyro:

- 1 green bell pepper, julienned
- 1 red onion, julienned
- 1 pound (454 g) skirt steak
- 4 pocketless pitas or naan bread
- 1 large ripe tomato, chopped
- 1 cucumber, sliced into thin half-moons
- 1 bunch microgreens, roughly chopped

Instructions:

1. Preheat your lightly oiled griddle to medium-high heat.

2. In a large bowl, whisk together the olive oil, lemon juice, minced garlic, oregano, paprika, salt, and a pinch of black pepper to create the marinade. Reserve 1 tablespoon (15 ml) of the marinade in a small bowl, then mix in the yogurt and water to make the yogurt sauce.

3. Add the julienned green bell pepper and onion to the bowl with the marinade. Using a slotted spoon, remove the veggies and set them aside. Place the skirt steak in the same marinade and toss until well coated. Let the steak sit in the marinade for a few minutes.

4. Place the bell peppers, onions, and marinated steak on the griddle. Cook the veggies for about 3 to 4 minutes until softened and slightly charred. Sear the steak for 4 to 8 minutes per side, or until it reaches your desired doneness. Once cooked, remove the steak and let it rest for 5 minutes.

5. While the steak is resting, warm the pitas or naan on the griddle for 1 to 2 minutes per side, until they begin to brown.

6. After resting, slice the steak against the grain. Assemble each gyro by adding steak, sautéed veggies, chopped tomato, cucumber, yogurt sauce, and a sprinkle of microgreens to each pita.

Sweet & Spicy Fig and Prosciutto Flatbreads

Making a flattop flatbread on the Blackstone couldn't be easier! We love recreating our favorite restaurant dishes at home, and this one was inspired by our beloved pie from Sixty Vines™. The combination of salty prosciutto, sweet figs, and hot honey creates a flavor explosion that you won't want to miss!

Makes 2 Flatbreads

Ingredients:

- 1 (2-pack) premade artisan flatbreads
- ½ cup (120 ml) Alfredo sauce
- ½ cup (57 g) shredded mozzarella cheese
- 2 ounces (56 g) smoked prosciutto
- ¼ cup (25 g) grated Parmesan cheese, plus extra for serving
- 4 tablespoons (60 ml) fig preserves, divided
- ½ cup (120 ml) water
- 2 cups (40 g) arugula
- 2 tablespoons (30 ml) hot honey
- Crushed red pepper flakes for serving

Instructions:

1. Preheat your griddle to medium-high heat. Lightly oil the hot griddle and place the flatbreads on it. Allow them to brown for about 3 minutes on each side.

2. Once the flatbreads are nicely browned, remove them from the heat. Spread ¼ cup (60 ml) of Alfredo sauce evenly over the top of each flatbread, leaving the edges clear. Next, sprinkle ¼ cup (29 g) of shredded mozzarella cheese over each flatbread, followed by 1 ounce (28 g) of smoked prosciutto, distributing it evenly. Finish with 2 tablespoons (13 g) of grated Parmesan cheese and dollop small teaspoons of fig preserves around the flatbread.

3. Place the flatbreads on a warming rack over the griddle to keep them from burning while the toppings warm up and the cheese melts. Pour the water onto the hot griddle to create steam, then close the hood or dome. Let them cook for 6 to 8 minutes, or until the cheese has melted and everything is heated through.

4. Once melted, remove the flatbreads from the heat. Top each flatbread with 1 cup (20 g) of arugula and drizzle 1 tablespoon (15 ml) of hot honey over the top. For extra flavor, add additional grated Parmesan cheese and crushed red pepper flakes to taste.

5. Slice and enjoy this delightful medley of flavors!

Smoky BBQ Pulled Pork Naan Pizzas

BBQ, pizza, and the Blackstone—what more could you want? One of my family's favorite ways to enjoy leftover BBQ is by whipping up these delicious flatbread pizzas. Using premade naan as the crust allows us to load on our favorite toppings without worrying about undercooked dough.

Makes 2 Flatbread Pizzas

Ingredients:

◄ 2 garlic naans

◄ 2 cups (498 g) leftover BBQ pulled pork

◄ 1 teaspoon BBQ seasoning, plus extra for garnish

◄ 2 tablespoons (30 ml) BBQ sauce, divided

◄ 2 ounces (56 g) shredded mozzarella cheese, divided

◄ ¼ teaspoon parsley flakes

◄ ¼ cup (60 ml) water

Instructions:

1. Preheat your lightly oiled griddle to medium-high heat. Once the griddle is hot, place the naan on it. Flip the naan every 30 seconds until they start to brown slightly, about 2 to 3 minutes per side.

2. After browning the naan, move them to a raised warming rack to cook indirectly for the remainder of the process.

3. Now, add the leftover pulled pork to the lightly oiled griddle over medium-high heat. Stir continuously until the pork begins to warm through and release moisture. After about 4 to 5 minutes, the edges should start to get crispy. Around the 3-minute mark, sprinkle about a teaspoon of BBQ seasoning over the pork for added flavor. Once the pork reaches your desired crispness, turn off the burner but keep the pork warm using residual heat.

4. Spread 1 tablespoon (15 ml) of your favorite BBQ sauce on each naan, using a silicone brush to ensure an even layer while leaving some space around the edges for the crust

5. Sprinkle about ½ ounce (14 g) of shredded mozzarella cheese on each sauced naan. Distribute half of the warmed pulled pork onto each flatbread evenly.

6. Top the pulled pork with the remaining 1 ounce (28 g) of shredded mozzarella cheese. Season each pizza with a ¼ teaspoon of BBQ seasoning and a dash of parsley flakes.

7. Prepare your dome or hood by placing the water around the warming rack on the griddle. Cover the pizzas with the hood or dome. The steam created by the water will help melt the cheese. After about a minute, lift the hood to check the cheese. If it hasn't melted to your liking, you can steam it a bit longer.

8. Once the cheese is melted, remove the pizzas from the warming rack and slice them into your desired portions.

Big Mac Fusion Flatbread Pizza

Combining pizza and the Big Mac is a dream come true for anyone who grew up loving these classic flavors! This fun twist brings all the iconic ingredients of the Big Mac into a delicious flatbread pizza, and it's all made effortlessly on your Blackstone. You're going to love this fusion!

Makes 2 Flatbread Pizzas

Ingredients:

Big Mac Sauce:

- 1 cup (240 ml) Duke's Mayonnaise
- ¼ cup (60 ml) ketchup
- ¼ cup (60 g) sweet relish
- 1 tablespoon (15 ml) yellow mustard
- 2 tablespoons (14 g) onion powder
- 1 teaspoon vinegar

Big Mac'N Pizza:

- ½ pound (226 g) lean ground beef
- Pinch of salt and freshly ground black pepper
- 1 (2-pack) premade artisan flatbreads
- Toasted sesame seeds
- 8 slices American cheese, cut into quarters
- 1 small onion, minced
- 20 dill pickle slices
- 2 tablespoons (30 ml) water
- ½ cup (35 g) shredded iceberg lettuce

Instructions:

1. Start by preparing the Big Mac sauce. In a bowl, combine the mayonnaise, ketchup, sweet relish, mustard, onion powder, and vinegar. Mix well until fully combined. Transfer the sauce to a squeeze bottle and chill in the refrigerator until ready to use.

2. Preheat your lightly oiled griddle to medium-high heat. Once hot, add the ground beef and cook, breaking it up into small pieces. Season with salt and pepper. Cook for about 7 to 8 minutes, or until the beef is browned and no longer pink. Drain any excess grease and set the beef aside.

3. Clean the griddle and lightly re-oil it. Place the flatbreads on the griddle, top-side down, and let them brown for 2 to 3 minutes. Flip the flatbreads over and sprinkle toasted sesame seeds on the tops to achieve that authentic Big Mac look. Let the bottom toast for another 2 to 3 minutes before removing the flatbreads from the heat.

4. Drizzle each flatbread with the Big Mac sauce, leaving about a 1-inch (2.5-cm) border for the crust. Divide the browned beef evenly between the flatbreads. Add half of the cheese slices to each flatbread, followed by the remaining beef. Distribute half of the minced onion and pickle slices over the top of each flatbread.

5. Place the flatbreads on a warming rack over the medium-high griddle. Pour the water around the warming rack and close the hood or dome over the top. This will create steam to help melt the cheese, which should take about 4 to 5 minutes. Once the cheese has melted, remove the flatbreads from the heat.

6. Top each pizza with shredded iceberg lettuce and drizzle with additional Big Mac sauce. Slice into pieces and serve hot!

Mini Zesty Naan Pizza Bites

This recipe is perfect for getting the kids involved in the kitchen! These zesty, cheesy pizza bites make for fantastic appetizers, party snacks, or even a main course. We've enjoyed them during movie nights, and they never disappoint. While this version features pepperoni, feel free to customize it with your favorite toppings and dipping sauces.

Makes 15–20 Mini Pizzas

Ingredients:

- ◄ 24 ounces (680 g) tomato pizza sauce
- ◄ 2 tablespoons (30 ml) extra virgin olive oil
- ◄ 7 ounces (200 g) Stonefire Naan Dippers (or any mini naan)
- ◄ 16 ounces (454 g) shredded mozzarella cheese
- ◄ 4 ounces (113 g) pepperoni
- ◄ 2 tablespoons (30 ml) water
- ◄ Italian seasoning for garnish

Instructions:

1. Preheat one side of your lightly oiled Blackstone griddle to medium-high heat and the other side to medium. Pour the pizza sauce into a pot and place it on the medium-high side of the griddle. Stir the sauce every minute, adjusting the heat as necessary. Once it begins to bubble, reduce the heat to low.

2. On the medium-heat side of the griddle, spread out the olive oil. Lay down the mini naan pieces and cook them for 2 to 3 minutes on each side, until they are lightly browned. Remove the naan and place them on a warming rack.

3. Set the warming rack over a baking sheet to catch any drips during the next step. Spoon some of the warmed pizza sauce onto each naan piece. Top with shredded mozzarella cheese and your desired amount of pepperoni. Carefully lift the loaded warming rack off the baking sheet and place it directly on the griddle. Increase the heat to medium-high. Pour the water onto the griddle near the warming rack to create steam. Close the hood or place a dome over the warming rack to help the cheese melt.

4. After about 3 to 4 minutes, use tongs to remove the naan pizza bites from the warming rack once the cheese is melted. Sprinkle Italian seasoning over the top.

5. Serve the pizza bites warm on a platter, accompanied by a bowl of warmed pizza sauce in the center for dipping.

Bacon Ranch Chicken Crunch Flatbreads

With just a couple of tortillas on hand, you can whip up all sorts of delicious griddle pizzas on the Blackstone. Feel free to mix and match sauces, cheeses, proteins, and veggies to create your perfect pizza. These cook up incredibly fast, making them a fun way for the whole family to get involved in the kitchen. You can use leftover rotisserie chicken or prepare some mayo-marinated chicken breasts for this recipe.

Makes 2 Pizzas

Ingredients:

- 8 slices of bacon
- 2 burrito-sized flour tortillas (or low-carb tortillas)
- ½ cup (120 g) plus 4 tablespoons (60 g) ranch dressing, divided
- 4 cups (880 g) shredded rotisserie chicken
- ½ red onion, thinly sliced
- 2 cups (226 g) shredded mozzarella cheese
- Fresh parsley, chopped for garnish

Instructions:

1. Start by setting your Blackstone griddle to low heat. Add the bacon slices to the griddle, cooking them slowly while flipping every minute. This method helps achieve perfectly crispy bacon without burning. After about 8 to 10 minutes, remove the bacon when it reaches your desired crispness. It will continue to crisp as it cools. Once cooled, crumble the bacon into pieces.

2. Scrape any excess bacon grease from the griddle and increase the heat to medium-low. Place the tortillas on the griddle, flipping them after 1 to 2 minutes.

3. Now it's time to build your pizzas! Spread ¼ cup (60 g) of ranch dressing on each tortilla, leaving a 1-inch (2.5 cm) border around the edge to form a crust. Top with shredded chicken, red onion slices, crumbled bacon, and a generous sprinkle of mozzarella cheese.

4. If you have a warming rack, place the pizzas on it and turn the griddle up to medium-high heat. Close the hood or dome over the pizzas. They'll be ready to remove once the cheese is melted, which should take about 5 minutes.

5. If you don't have a warming rack, reduce the griddle heat to low, close the lid, and cook until the cheese melts, approximately 7 to 10 minutes.

6. Once the cheese has melted, garnish the pizzas with chopped parsley and drizzle with the remaining 4 tablespoons (60 g) of ranch dressing. Slice and serve hot!

Chapter 6 Griddled Pastas

Zesty Italian Ravioli Skillet

When it comes to quick weeknight meals on the Blackstone, we're always on the lookout for easy options. With busy schedules filled with sports, practices, and meetings, finding time for a delicious meal can be tough. This simple pasta dish cooked on the griddle is a fantastic choice for those hectic evenings or for a relaxed weekend gathering with friends and family.

Makes 4 Servings

Ingredients:

- 3 tablespoons (45 ml) extra virgin olive oil, divided
- 20 ounces (567 g) premade four-cheese ravioli
- 1 green bell pepper, julienned
- 1 red bell pepper, julienned
- 1 medium white or yellow onion, julienned
- 19 ounces (538 g) sweet Italian sausage, sliced
- 2 cloves garlic, minced
- 1 (16-ounce [473-ml]) bottle Blackstone's Loaded Italian Sear and Serve sauce
- Pinch of parsley flakes for garnish
- 3 tablespoons (20 g) grated Parmesan cheese for garnish

Instructions:

1. Begin by boiling a large pot of water on the Blackstone set to high or on a side burner. Add 1 tablespoon (15 ml) of olive oil to the water. Once it reaches a rolling boil, add the ravioli and cook for about 2 minutes (or follow the package instructions). Drain the ravioli and set aside.

2. Heat your lightly oiled Blackstone to medium-high. Add the julienned peppers and onion to the griddle. Sauté the vegetables for about 3 minutes until they start to soften. Then, add the sliced sausage and cook for 5 to 6 minutes until browned and cooked through.

3. Stir in the minced garlic and sauté for 1 to 2 minutes until fragrant. Drizzle in the remaining 2 tablespoons (30 ml) of olive oil, then gently add the cooked ravioli. Toss everything together every minute or so, cooking until the ravioli begins to brown, about 5 more minutes.

4. Shake the Loaded Italian Sear and Serve sauce well before adding about half of the bottle to the mixture. If the pasta appears dry, add more sauce. Toss everything together and cook for an additional 2 to 3 minutes until well combined.

5. Transfer the pasta mixture to a serving platter or large bowl. Garnish with parsley flakes and grated Parmesan cheese. Serve warm and enjoy!

Betty's Classic Chicken Alfredo Penne

No discussion of pasta on the Blackstone would be complete without mentioning Desirée Ruberti, affectionately known as "Blackstone Betty." She continuously challenges the conventional ideas of what can be cooked on the Blackstone. Betty's legendary Family Style Sunday meals often feature her entire family in her online videos and livestreams, creating a fun and engaging cooking experience. This recipe is my tribute to her dedication and contributions as part of the Blackstone Griddle Crew and to all of #GriddleNation.

Makes 4 to 6 Servings

Ingredients:

- ◀ 1 pound (454 g) penne rigate pasta
- ◀ 2 tablespoons (30 ml) extra virgin olive oil, divided
- ◀ 1 pound (454 g) chicken breast cutlets, pounded to ¼ inch (6 mm) thickness
- ◀ 1½ tablespoons (8 g) Blackstone Tutto Italiano seasoning (or your favorite Italian seasoning)
- ◀ 1 small white onion, finely chopped
- ◀ 3 cloves garlic, minced
- ◀ 5 cups (150 g) baby spinach
- ◀ 1 (8.5-ounce [241-g]) jar sun-dried tomatoes in oil, julienned
- ◀ 15 ounces (425 g) Alfredo sauce
- ◀ 8 ounces (226 g) Parmesan cheese wedge, divided

Instructions:

1. Begin by bringing a large pot of salted water to a boil on the Blackstone set to high or on a side burner. Cook the penne rigate for 8 to 9 minutes until it reaches your preferred tenderness (or follow the package directions). Reserve 2 cups (480 ml) of the pasta water, then strain the pasta.

2. Heat your griddle to medium-high and lightly coat it with 1 tablespoon (15 ml) of olive oil. Season both sides of the chicken cutlets with the Blackstone Tutto Italiano seasoning. Once the oil begins to shimmer, add the chicken to the griddle. Cook each side for 3 to 4 minutes, or until the internal temperature reaches 160°F (70°C). Remove the chicken from the griddle and let it rest for 5 minutes before slicing it into bite-sized pieces.

3. Add the remaining 1 tablespoon (15 ml) of olive oil to the griddle. Toss in the chopped onion and sauté for 3 to 4 minutes until it becomes translucent and soft. Stir in the minced garlic and cook for an additional 30 seconds until fragrant. Add the baby spinach and the jar of julienned sun-dried tomatoes to the onion mixture, tossing frequently for 2 to 3 minutes until the spinach wilts.

4. Incorporate the cooked pasta and Alfredo sauce into the spinach mixture, stirring until everything is well combined. Lower the griddle temperature to low and grate half of the Parmesan cheese over the pasta. Stir to blend the flavors.

5. Allow the pasta to simmer on the griddle for 4 to 5 minutes to meld the flavors. If the sauce appears too thick, use some of the reserved pasta water to achieve your desired consistency.

6. Serve hot, topped with additional freshly grated Parmesan cheese to taste.

Garden Fresh Tortellini Toss

My friend Todd Toven over at Blackstone has popularized a delightful dish called "Toddeloni," which features tortellini cooked on the griddle! Similar to the ravioli dish in this chapter, it's a quick and versatile meal that can be customized based on what you have at home. Feel free to add or omit ingredients as you see fit. This meat-free version is perfect for any vegetarians visiting or living with you.

Makes 4 Servings

Ingredients:

- 3 tablespoons (45 ml) extra virgin olive oil, divided
- 20 ounces (567 g) premade mixed-cheese tortellini
- 1 medium white or yellow onion, julienned
- 8 ounces (226 g) baby portabella mushrooms, cleaned and sliced
- 2 cloves garlic, minced
- 1 (16-ounce [473 ml]) bottle Blackstone Garlic Parmesan Sear and Serve sauce
- 2½ cups (75 g) baby spinach
- 3 tablespoons (20 g) grated Parmesan cheese for serving

Instructions:

1. Begin by boiling a large pot of water on the Blackstone set to high heat or on a side burner. Add 1 tablespoon (15 ml) of olive oil to the water. Once it reaches a rolling boil, add the tortellini and cook for about 2 minutes until tender (or follow the package directions). Drain the tortellini and set aside.

2. Preheat your lightly oiled Blackstone to medium heat. Add the julienned onion and sliced mushrooms to the griddle. Sauté for about 3 minutes until they begin to soften. Then, add the minced garlic and cook for an additional 1 to 2 minutes until fragrant.

3. Drizzle the remaining 2 tablespoons (30 ml) of olive oil over the mixture, followed by the cooked tortellini. Gently toss everything every minute or so, allowing the pasta to brown and sear for about 5 minutes.

4. Shake the bottle of Garlic Parmesan Sear and Serve sauce and pour about half of it over the pasta. If the mixture appears dry, add more sauce as needed. Stir in the baby spinach and cook for another 2 to 3 minutes until the spinach wilts.

5. Transfer the tortellini and vegetable mixture to a serving platter or large bowl. Top with grated Parmesan cheese and serve warm.

Sizzling Blackstone Baked Ziti Extravaganza

As a child, baked ziti was one of my absolute favorite meals. This fun and flavorful griddled version on the Blackstone is just as delicious, if not more so! Feel free to customize the recipe by adding mushrooms, marinated artichokes, or any other veggies you love.

Makes 4 Servings

Ingredients:

- 16 ounces (454 g) ziti pasta
- 1 pound (454 g) ground Italian sausage
- ½ medium yellow onion, diced
- 1 green bell pepper, diced
- 2 cloves garlic, minced
- 1 teaspoon Meat Church Garlic and Herb seasoning (or your favorite Italian seasoning)
- Pinch of crushed red pepper flakes (optional)
- 32 ounces (907 g) marinara sauce
- ¾ cup (85 g) shredded Parmesan cheese, for serving
- 2 tablespoons (3 g) fresh basil, chopped, for garnish
- Garlic bread, for serving

Instructions:

1. Begin by boiling a large pot of water on the Blackstone or on a side burner. Cook the ziti according to the package directions, but slightly undercook it—about 8 minutes. Drain the pasta and set aside.

2. Heat your lightly oiled griddle to medium. Once hot, add the ground Italian sausage. Cook for 7 to 8 minutes, breaking it into small pieces until fully browned and no pink remains.

3. Add the diced onion and bell pepper to the sausage. Sauté until the vegetables soften and develop a bit of color, about 4 to 5 minutes.

4. Create a small well in the center of the sausage mixture and add the minced garlic. Cook for 30 seconds to 1 minute, or until fragrant. Stir the garlic into the sausage mixture and season with the Meat Church Garlic and Herb seasoning and optional crushed red pepper flakes.

5. Reduce the heat to low on all burners. Gently fold in the marinara sauce and cooked pasta, tossing until everything is well combined and the sauce starts to simmer, approximately 5 minutes.

6. Serve the ziti hot, garnished with shredded Parmesan cheese, fresh basil, and a side of garlic bread for a delightful meal.

Crispy Griddled Chicken Parm Perfection

I have a soft spot for chicken parmesan—it's my guilty pleasure whenever I visit an Italian restaurant. The delightful contrast of crispy chicken, savory sauce, and gooey melted cheese is simply irresistible. This version employs shallow frying techniques, making it a favorite in our household! If you're a cheese lover, feel free to pile on the mozzarella to your heart's content.

Makes 4 Servings

Ingredients:

- 4 boneless, skinless chicken breasts
- Pinch of salt and freshly ground black pepper
- 1¾ cups (170 g) pork panko or regular panko breadcrumbs
- 3 ounces (85 g) grated Parmigiano Reggiano cheese, divided
- 2 teaspoons (5 g) Meat Church Garlic and Herb seasoning (or garlic salt)
- 3 large eggs
- 2 tablespoons (30 ml) water
- 1 cup (240 ml) canola oil
- 24 ounces (680 g) spaghetti sauce
- 12 ounces (340 g) spaghetti noodles, cooked

Instructions:

1. Start by pounding the chicken breasts until they are about ¼ inch (6 mm) thick. This ensures even cooking on the griddle. Season both sides of the chicken with a pinch of salt and black pepper.
2. In a large shallow bowl, combine the pork panko, 2 ounces (56 g) of grated Parmigiano Reggiano, and the Meat Church Garlic and Herb seasoning. This will be your dry dredge. In another shallow bowl, whisk together the eggs and water to create the wet dredge.
3. Dip each flattened chicken breast into the wet mixture, ensuring all sides are coated. Next, transfer the chicken to the dry dredge, flipping to cover all sides thoroughly. Repeat this for each breast.
4. Preheat the griddle to medium-high heat. Pour the canola oil into the center of the griddle for frying. Once you see wisps of white smoke rising, add the coated chicken breasts to the oil.
5. While the chicken is frying, heat the spaghetti sauce in a separate pan on the medium-high griddle, stirring occasionally until warmed through.
6. Cook each chicken breast for 6 to 8 minutes per side, or until golden brown and crispy. The internal temperature should reach 165°F (75°C). You may need to flip the chicken several times for even cooking. Once done, remove from heat and let the chicken rest for a moment before slicing.
7. To serve, place 3 ounces (85 g) of cooked spaghetti on each plate. Top with a generous ladle of warm spaghetti sauce, followed by slices of the chicken parmesan. Drizzle with more sauce and finish with freshly grated Parmigiano Reggiano.
8. Present this delicious meal to your friends and family, and enjoy the admiration for the versatility of the Blackstone Griddle!

Chapter 7 Fried rice and vermicelli noodles

Speedy Shrimp Fried Rice Griddle Fiesta

Fried rice can often require extensive prep, but this quick and easy version is perfect for a busy night. Using shortcuts, you can whip up a delicious meal in just minutes on your Blackstone! I'm sure you'll love how simple and tasty it is.

Makes 4 Servings

Ingredients:

- 2 tablespoons (30 ml) canola oil (or any cooking oil of your choice)
- 2 (16-ounce [454-g]) bags of frozen vegetable fried rice (I recommend Trader Joe's™)
- 1 pound (454 g) raw, peeled shrimp (tails removed)
- 12 ounces (340 g) broccoli slaw
- 4 roma tomatoes, quartered
- ½ cup (25 g) chopped green onions
- ¼ cup (60 ml) Bachan's Japanese BBQ sauce (or teriyaki sauce)
- Toasted sesame seeds, for garnish

Instructions:

1. Preheat your griddle to high and pour in the cooking oil.
2. Once the oil is hot and shimmering, add both bags of frozen fried rice. Stir every 30 seconds, allowing it to cook for about 2 minutes.
3. Incorporate the raw shrimp and broccoli slaw into the rice, mixing well to combine.
4. Continue cooking for an additional 3 minutes, stirring frequently. Then, add the quartered tomatoes, chopped green onions, and Japanese BBQ sauce. Stir continuously until the shrimp are fully cooked, approximately 3 to 4 minutes.
5. Finish with a sprinkle of toasted sesame seeds and serve hot.

Crispy Tuna Wonton Nacho Fusion

Get ready to elevate your culinary experience with this delightful fusion of sushi and nachos. This recipe features crispy fried wonton chips topped with fresh, flavorful ahi tuna. It's a fun dish that combines textures and tastes, and I'm excited for you to try it!

Makes 2 Servings

Ingredients:

- 2 (6-ounce [170-g]) sushi-grade ahi tuna fillets
- 2 tablespoons (30 ml) soy sauce, plus extra for serving
- 4 tablespoons (10 g) Everything But The Bagel seasoning
- 1 cup (240 ml) avocado oil, divided
- 12 ounces (340 g) wonton wrappers, cut diagonally in half
- 2 jalapeños, sliced
- Squeezable Japanese mayonnaise
- Squeezable guacamole
- ½ cup (8 g) chopped cilantro
- Sriracha, for serving

Instructions:

1. Start by patting the ahi tuna fillets dry with a paper towel. Drizzle soy sauce over all sides to help the seasoning adhere. Generously coat the tuna with Everything But The Bagel seasoning, using about 2 tablespoons (5 g) per fillet.

2. Heat 2 tablespoons (30 ml) of avocado oil on the griddle until you see wisps of smoke. Carefully place the tuna on the hot oil and sear each side for about 60 seconds. This quick sear will create a crust while keeping the inside raw. Remove the tuna from the griddle and set aside to cool.

3. Once the tuna has cooled, cut it into 1-inch (2.5-cm) cubes. For a refreshing touch, chill the cubes in the fridge while you prepare the wonton chips.

4. Lower the heat to medium and add the remaining avocado oil to the griddle. Shallow-fry the halved wonton wrappers in the hot oil, flipping every 30 seconds. Fry until golden brown, about 3 to 4 minutes. Transfer the fried wontons to a paper towel-lined plate. Continue frying until you have about 24 chips (12 chips per serving). As the wontons fry, sauté the sliced jalapeños on the side of the griddle for about 2 minutes until softened and browned, then remove them from the heat.

5. Divide the crispy wonton chips between two plates. Top each plate with the chilled seared tuna cubes, sautéed jalapeños, a drizzle of Japanese mayonnaise, dollops of guacamole, and a sprinkle of chopped cilantro.

6. Offer sriracha and extra soy sauce on the side for dipping. Dive into this unique and flavorful dish!

Griddle-Master's Pad Thai Feast

This recipe is a tribute to Chef Jet Tila's amazing Pad Thai from his cookbook 101 Thai Dishes You Need to Cook Before You Die. Chef Tila is one of my culinary heroes, known for his appearances on the Food Network.
Creating dishes like this on the griddle gives me immense joy, especially ones you might not expect to cook on a flat top. Discovering how to make Pad Thai this way has been a game changer for us. Once you try this version, you'll find yourself craving takeout a lot less!

Makes 4 Servings

Ingredients:

Noodles:
- 6–8 cups (620–960 g) medium rice stick noodles (you can substitute with fresh rice noodles)

Sauce:
- ½ cup (120 ml) fish sauce
- ½ cup (120 g) white sugar
- 6 tablespoons (90 ml) tamarind concentrate
- 2 tablespoons (30 ml) fresh lime juice
- 2 tablespoons (30 ml) rice vinegar

Pad Thai:
- 4 tablespoons (60 ml) avocado or canola oil, divided
- 4 cloves garlic, minced
- 4 tablespoons (30 g) shredded sweetened radish
- 2 teaspoons (4 g) shrimp powder with chili
- 1 cup (250 g) baked tofu, diced small
- 4 eggs
- 20 large to medium shrimp, raw, peeled and deveined

- 2 tablespoons (14 g) smoked paprika, for color
- 6 scallions, julienned, divided
- ½ cup (73 g) chopped dry-roasted unsalted peanuts, divided
- 2 cups (90 g) bean sprouts, for garnish
- 1 lime, for garnish (optional)
- Chili paste or sriracha, for serving (optional)

Instructions:

1. Begin by soaking the dry rice noodles in hot water for about an hour. This will help the noodles become pliable. After soaking, drain them well, saving a cup (240 ml) of the soaking water. If using fresh rice noodles, you can skip this step.

2. For the sauce, whisk together the fish sauce, white sugar, tamarind concentrate, lime juice, and rice vinegar in a bowl until the sugar dissolves. Set aside for later use.

3. Preheat your griddle to high heat. For a larger griddle, such as a 36-inch (91-cm) Blackstone, turn on three zones while leaving one side off to prevent burning ingredients. Once heated, add 2 tablespoons (30 ml) of avocado oil and spread it around.

4. When the oil starts to emit white smoke, toss in the minced garlic and stir for about 15 seconds until fragrant. Add the radish, shrimp powder, and diced tofu, stirring for another minute.

5. Push the cooked ingredients to the side of the griddle that is off. Add the remaining 2 tablespoons (30 ml) of avocado oil to the hot side. Once heated, crack the eggs onto the griddle, breaking the yolks and allowing them to fry. After 30 seconds, fold the eggs into the mixture on the cooler side.

6. Add the shrimp to the hot side of the griddle, stirring for 30 seconds to a minute. As they change color, mix everything back on the hot side for another 3 to 5 minutes, or until the shrimp are pink and curled.

7. Incorporate the soaked or fresh noodles, stirring everything together, and cook for 3 to 4 minutes until the noodles begin to soften. Gradually pour in the sauce you prepared along with the paprika, ensuring to add it slowly to give the noodles time to absorb it. Stir for about 3 minutes until the sauce is well distributed and the noodles soak it up.

8. Mix in half of the scallions and half of the peanuts, ensuring everything is well combined. Turn off the heat.

9. Serve the Pad Thai on four plates, garnishing with additional scallions, chopped peanuts, and bean sprouts. A squeeze of fresh lime just before serving enhances the dish beautifully.

10. For an extra kick, feel free to add chili paste or sriracha either during cooking or at the table. Enjoy your delightful Pad Thai fusion!

Bulgogi Udon Stir-Fry Sensation

I was genuinely amazed at how simple and delicious this recipe turned out to be. Marinating the beef and vegetables in advance really made dinner prep a breeze on a busy weeknight, and cooking everything on the Blackstone made it even more efficient. The udon noodles absorb all the flavors from the marinade, resulting in an incredible taste in every bite!

Makes 2 Servings

Ingredients:

Bulgogi Marinade:

- ◀ 4 tablespoons (60 ml) soy sauce
- ◀ 1 tablespoon (15 ml) sesame oil
- ◀ 2 tablespoons (30 ml) mirin
- ◀ 1 tablespoon (14 g) brown sugar
- ◀ 1 tablespoon (15 ml) honey
- ◀ 6 cloves minced garlic
- ◀ Pinch of ground black pepper

Bulgogi Beef:

- ◀ 11 ounces (300 g) sliced beef rib eye
- ◀ ½ medium onion, sliced
- ◀ ½ cup (67 g) julienned carrot

Noodles:

- ◀ 2 tablespoons (30 ml) vegetable oil
- ◀ 2 (14-ounce [392-g]) packs udon noodles
- ◀ 1 tablespoon (15 ml) oyster sauce

- ◀ ½ cup (40 g) shiitake mushrooms, sliced
- ◀ 2 green onions, chopped

- ◀ Pinch of toasted sesame seeds, for garnish
- ◀ 1 thinly sliced green onion, for garnish

Instructions:

1. Start by whisking together the soy sauce, sesame oil, mirin, brown sugar, honey, minced garlic, and black pepper in a bowl to create the marinade.

2. In a large zip-top bag, combine the sliced beef, onion, carrot, shiitake mushrooms, and green onions. Pour the marinade over the mixture, seal the bag, and mix well. Let it marinate for at least 20 minutes or up to overnight in the refrigerator. When you're ready to cook, allow the bag to sit out at room temperature for about 10 minutes. This step helps avoid shocking the griddle with cold liquid, which can warp the surface.

3. Heat the vegetable oil on the griddle over medium-high heat. Once hot, carefully add the marinated bulgogi mixture. Cook for about 3 to 4 minutes, stirring occasionally, until the vegetables are tender and the beef is browned.

4. Add the udon noodles and oyster sauce to the pan, stirring everything together and allowing it to fry for an additional 2 to 3 minutes.

5. Divide the bulgogi noodle mixture into two bowls. Garnish with toasted sesame seeds and slices of green onion for a fresh finish.

Enjoy this delightful meal that packs a punch of flavor with minimal effort!

Spicy Thai Basil Pork with Fried Egg Bliss

Here's a vibrant dish inspired by Chef Jet Tila that's sure to please your palate! This quick and flavorful meal is perfect for the Blackstone, combining spicy and sweet elements that will make your taste buds dance. The addition of fried eggs takes it to another level, so let's get that griddle heated up and dive in!

Makes 4 Servings

Ingredients:

- 3 tablespoons (45 ml) canola oil (sub other high-temperature cooking oil)
- 16 ounces (454 g) ground pork
- 4 cloves garlic, minced
- 2–4 fresh Thai chilies, minced
- 1 teaspoon ground black pepper
- 2 cups (220 g) green beans, cut into small pieces
- 1 cup (240 ml) chicken stock
- ¼ cup (60 ml) Bachan's Japanese BBQ sauce (sub your favorite Japanese sauce)
- 4 large eggs
- 2 cups (48 g) whole Thai sweet basil leaves, loosely packed
- Cooked jasmine rice, for serving

Instructions:

1. Heat your lightly oiled griddle to high temperature. Once it's hot, pour in the canola oil and spread it evenly with your spatula. Add the ground pork to the griddle, making sure to spread it out. Let it cook undisturbed for about 2 minutes, then flip it and let it brown on the other side for another 2 minutes. After that, break the pork into bite-sized pieces.

2. Stir in the minced garlic, Thai chilies, black pepper, and green beans with the pork. Cook this mixture for about 2 to 3 minutes, stirring frequently until the green beans begin to char slightly.

3. Gradually pour in the chicken stock while using your spatula to scrape up any bits of pork or garlic that may be stuck to the griddle. Be careful to keep the stock from running into the grease trap. Watch as the chicken stock comes to a boil, then allow it to reduce by half, stirring every 30 seconds.

4. Mix in the Bachan's Japanese BBQ sauce and stir until well combined. As the sauce incorporates, it will start to thicken.

5. On another section of the griddle set to medium heat, fry the eggs until they reach your desired doneness. Set them aside once cooked.

6. In the final 30 seconds of cooking, add the Thai sweet basil leaves to the thickening sauce, allowing them to wilt.

7. Serve the flavorful Bangin' Basil Pork over a bed of jasmine rice, and top each portion with a perfectly fried egg. Enjoy this delightful fusion of flavors!

Sizzling Pepper Steak Stir-Fry Sensation

Get ready to discover why I call this dish Poppin' Pepper Steak Stir-Fry! It's a quick and fiery recipe that shines on a hot Blackstone. As always, it's essential to have all your ingredients prepped and within reach before you begin cooking. Once you start, there's no time for slicing the steak!

Growing up, pepper steak was my favorite dish, and I loved the bold flavors and the larger pieces of steak and peppers, which made it easier for me to practice using chopsticks. If you haven't used chopsticks much, I encourage you to give it a try with this dish—you might surprise yourself!

Makes 4 Servings

Ingredients:

- ◀ 1 tablespoon (15 ml) canola oil, divided
- ◀ 1 green bell pepper, julienned
- ◀ 1 red bell pepper, julienned
- ◀ 1½ pounds (680 g) flank or sirloin steak, thinly sliced
- ◀ Pinch of salt and ground black pepper
- ◀ 2 teaspoons (4 g) minced garlic
- ◀ 1 teaspoon minced ginger
- ◀ ¼ cup (60 ml) soy sauce
- ◀ 1½ tablespoons (22 g) sugar
- ◀ 1½ tablespoons (12 g) cornstarch
- ◀ ¼ cup (60 ml) water
- ◀ Cooked white or brown rice

Instructions:

1. Start by setting your griddle to high heat and adding 1 teaspoon of canola oil.

2. Toss in the green and red bell peppers. Stir the peppers every 30 seconds or so. After about 3 to 4 minutes, they should become tender. Remove them from the griddle and set aside.

3. Season the sliced steak with a pinch of salt and black pepper. Add the remaining oil to the griddle and place the steak on it. Stir every 30 seconds, allowing the steak to develop a nice sear. After 5 to 6 minutes, the steak should be lightly browned.

4. Add the minced garlic and ginger to the steak, stirring continuously until fragrant, which should take about 30 seconds. Reintroduce the peppers to the griddle and mix them with the steak.

5. In a bowl, whisk together the soy sauce, sugar, cornstarch, and water until smooth. Pour this sauce over the steak and peppers, stirring continuously for 2 to 3 minutes until the sauce thickens. Remove the mixture from the griddle.

6. Serve the delicious stir-fry over cooked white or brown rice. Enjoy this vibrant dish!

Smoked Salmon Okonomiyaki Pancakes

Get ready for a delightful Japanese-inspired dinner at our place! Okonomiyaki translates to "grilled as you like it," allowing for endless variations with different vegetables, meats, and seasonings. In my rendition, I've incorporated traditional ingredients alongside smoked salmon, creating a delicious pancake that will take your taste buds on an exciting journey!

Makes 2 Okonomiyaki

Ingredients:

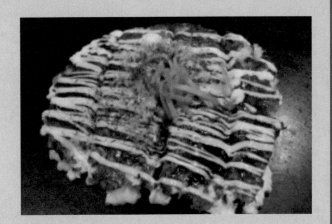

- 3 packed cups (210 g) finely shredded cabbage
- 1¼ cups (62 g) chopped scallions, about 1 bunch
- 1 cup (56 g) panko breadcrumbs
- ¾ teaspoon sea salt
- 3 eggs, beaten
- 1 tablespoon (15 ml) Japanese mayonnaise, for topping
- Sriracha, to taste, for topping
- Sesame seeds and Japanese furikake, for topping
- 4 ounces (113 g) smoked salmon, divided, for topping

Instructions:

1. In a large bowl, combine the shredded cabbage, chopped scallions, panko breadcrumbs, sea salt, and beaten eggs. Mix well until everything is evenly combined.

2. Preheat your medium-heat griddle and generously oil the surface. Scoop half of the mixture onto the griddle, shaping it into a large pancake. Repeat this process on another well-oiled griddle for the second okonomiyaki. Cook each pancake for 5 to 6 minutes on each side, allowing them to brown nicely before removing them from the heat.

3. After cooking, top each okonomiyaki with a drizzle of Japanese mayonnaise, a splash of sriracha, and a sprinkle of sesame seeds and furikake. Finally, layer 2 ounces (56 g) of smoked salmon on top (sushi-grade poke salmon would be a fantastic alternative).

4. Enjoy your homemade okonomiyaki and experience the wonderful flavors of Japan!

Chapter 8 Desserts

Campfire S'mores Quesadilla Treats

This quick and delightful dessert recipe is perfect for any impromptu backyard gathering or campsite hangout. Preparing it on the Blackstone allows you to enjoy all the delicious flavors of s'mores without the risks of flaming marshmallows flying around the campsite.

Makes 4 S'Mores Quesadillas

Ingredients:

- 1 cup (200 g) granulated sugar
- 4 tablespoons (32 g) ground cinnamon
- 4 tablespoons (57 g) unsalted butter, melted, divided
- 4 burrito-sized flour tortillas
- 1 pound (454 g) miniature marshmallows
- 12 ounces (340 g) semi-sweet chocolate chips
- 4 (14 g) sheets graham crackers, crushed into chunks

Instructions:

1. Begin by preheating your lightly oiled Blackstone griddle to medium-low heat. The size of your griddle will determine how many quesadillas you can prepare at once.

2. In a shallow dish that fits your tortilla when folded, mix the sugar and cinnamon together.

3. Brush one side of each tortilla with melted butter and place the buttered side down on the griddle. On one half of the tortilla, layer your desired amount of marshmallows, chocolate chips, and a sprinkle of crushed graham crackers.

4. Fold the tortilla over and flip it every 30 seconds or so, cooking until the chocolate and marshmallows melt, which should take about 2 to 3 minutes.

5. Once cooked, remove the quesadilla from the heat and brush both sides with more melted butter. Dip the buttered quesadilla into the cinnamon sugar mixture, flipping it to coat the outside evenly. Repeat for each quesadilla.

6. Slice each s'mores quesadilla into four triangles and serve them around the campfire or patio table, enjoying as these tasty treats quickly disappear!

Golden Griddled Peaches with Cinnamon Brioche Crumble and Brown Butter

I'm excited to reintroduce this recipe for my cookbook! This dish was a key entry in the Blackstone Great Griddle Off contest back in 2020, where it played a pivotal role in my journey to winning the Golden Spatula award.

Makes 4 Servings

Ingredients:

- Cinnamon Toast Crunch Brioche Crumb:
- 4 slices brioche bread, torn or pulsed into fine crumbs (about 2 cups [216 g] of crumbs)
- 4 tablespoons (57 g) salted butter, melted
- 4 tablespoons (60 g) cinnamon sugar

Brown Butter:

- 4 tablespoons (57 g) salted butter
- 2 tablespoons (30 ml) honey
- 1 teaspoon vanilla extract
- ½ teaspoon ground cinnamon

Griddled Peaches:

- 2 peaches, halved, peeled and pits removed
- 1 pint (473 ml) vanilla ice cream, for serving

Instructions:

1. To prepare the cinnamon toast crumbs, preheat your oven to 350°F (175°C). Line a baking sheet with parchment paper and add the brioche crumbs, melted butter, and cinnamon sugar. Toss everything together until the crumbs are well coated. Bake in the preheated oven for 10 to 15 minutes, or until the crumbs are toasted and golden brown.

2. For the brown butter, add the butter to a skillet over medium heat on the Blackstone. Allow the butter to cook, stirring frequently, until it turns a deep golden brown and emits a nutty aroma, about 3 to 4 minutes. Remove from heat and transfer the brown butter to a heat-proof bowl. Stir in the honey, vanilla extract, and ground cinnamon. This can be used right away or cooled completely and stored in the fridge for up to a week. If storing, let it come to room temperature before serving.

3. For the peaches, set your lightly oiled griddle to medium-high heat. Place the peach halves cut side down on the griddle. Cook until they are heated through and caramelized, about 6 to 7 minutes.

4. Serve the warm griddled peaches topped with a generous scoop of vanilla ice cream, drizzled with the brown butter, and sprinkled with the cinnamon toast brioche crumbs for a delightful finish. Enjoy this sweet and indulgent treat!

Crispy Griddled Cinnamon Rolls with Pecan Bliss

When it comes to desserts on the griddle, these smashed cinnamon rolls are as easy as they come! By flattening them out, they cook evenly and achieve a delightful crispy finish. They're perfect for a sweet treat after dinner or a delightful breakfast while camping.

Makes 10 Smashed Cinnamon Rolls

Ingredients:

- 2 (17.5-ounce [496-g]) cans Pillsbury Grands! Cinnamon Rolls with Cinnabon Cinnamon and Original Icing (sub any other canned cinnamon rolls)
- 6 tablespoons (85 g) cinnamon compound butter, divided (sub plain, unsalted butter)
- ½ cup (55 g) chopped pecans

Instructions:

1. Begin by heating your lightly oiled griddle to medium heat. Open the cans of cinnamon rolls and separate them. Leave the icing at room temperature to soften while you prepare the rolls.

2. Depending on the size of your griddle, you can determine how many cinnamon rolls to cook at once. Ensure there's enough space to smash them without them touching and to accommodate the pecans. On a 36-inch (91-cm) griddle, you should have ample room for everything.

3. Spread half of the cinnamon butter across the griddle surface. Place the cinnamon rolls on the buttered griddle with the flat sides down. To smash them flat, use parchment paper to avoid sticking. You might want to add a bit of butter to the parchment to prevent it from sticking as well. Once flattened, let them cook until the bottoms turn golden brown, approximately 2 to 3 minutes. Flip them over and let the other side brown for another 2 to 3 minutes.

4. While the cinnamon rolls are cooking, add the remaining butter to the griddle and toss in the chopped pecans. Stir the pecans every minute or so, and remove them when they are warm and fragrant.

5. After the cinnamon rolls are done, let them cool for about 2 minutes. In the meantime, mix the softened icing and warm pecans in a bowl until well combined.

6. Drizzle the pecan icing over the warm smashed cinnamon rolls and serve immediately! Enjoy this delectable treat!

Sweet Strawberry Basil Brie Melt with a Zesty Twist

The Blackstone Griddle is fantastic for creating grilled cheese, so why not turn it into a dessert? These sweet and cheesy sandwiches can be enjoyed any time of the day. The combination of sweet strawberries and zesty lemon harmonizes beautifully with the rich, savory brie.

Makes 4 Sandwiches

Ingredients:

- 1 cup (166 g) large strawberries, chopped
- 4 large basil leaves, sliced thin
- 1 teaspoon extra virgin olive oil
- ½ teaspoon balsamic vinegar
- ¼ teaspoon lemon zest
- Pinch of salt and ground black pepper
- 4 tablespoons (57 g) unsalted butter
- 8 thin slices sourdough baguette
- 8 ounces (226 g) Brie cheese

Instructions:

1. Start by preheating your lightly oiled griddle to medium-high heat. Once it's hot, add the chopped strawberries and let them cook for about 1 minute before stirring. Allow them to cook for another minute, then transfer the strawberries to a mixing bowl. Scrape any remnants off the griddle while keeping it on medium-high heat.

2. In the mixing bowl, combine the strawberries with the basil, olive oil, balsamic vinegar, lemon zest, and a pinch of salt and black pepper. Stir until everything is well mixed.

3. Butter one side of each slice of sourdough. Cut the brie cheese into quarters.

4. Place 4 of the sourdough slices on the hot griddle, buttered side down. Layer each slice with a quarter of the strawberry mixture and a quarter of the brie cheese. Top each with another slice of sourdough, buttered side up.

5. Close the hood or dome over the sandwiches. Cook for 3 to 4 minutes, until the bread turns golden brown. Carefully flip the sandwiches and cook until the other side is golden and the cheese has melted.

6. Serve the sandwiches warm and enjoy this delightful sweet treat!

Decadent Griddled Chocolate Cinnamon Toast

Get ready for a dessert that will leave you craving more! This quick and easy recipe can be prepared and cooked in under 10 minutes on the Blackstone, delivering a treat that is both simple and indulgent.

Makes 4 Treats

Ingredients:

- ◀ 8 slices whole grain bread
- ◀ 4 tablespoons (57 g) salted butter
- ◀ 1 cup (200 g) sugar
- ◀ 2½ tablespoons (20 g) ground cinnamon
- ◀ 8 ounces (226 g) semi-sweet or dark chocolate, chopped

Instructions:

1. Begin by preheating your lightly oiled griddle to medium heat. Toast the bread for about 1 to 2 minutes on each side until it begins to turn lightly golden.

2. Once toasted, spread butter on one side of each slice of warm bread. In a separate bowl, mix together the sugar and ground cinnamon. Generously sprinkle the buttered side of each slice with the cinnamon sugar mixture, saving some for later.

3. Place 4 of the buttered slices on the griddle, buttered side down. Distribute the chopped chocolate evenly on these slices and then top with the remaining 4 slices, ensuring the buttered side is facing up.

4. Cook the sandwiches for 2 to 3 minutes on each side, until both sides are golden brown and the chocolate has fully melted. Remove from heat and slice diagonally for serving.

5. Enjoy your warm, chocolatey treats!

Bananas Foster Griddle Melts with Creamy Cheese Bliss

You bet there are two incredible dessert grilled cheeses in this chapter! This recipe combines bananas, melty cheeses, and crunchy bread to create a delightful treat that's sure to make you swing with joy. So let's get to it and whip up this delicious dessert on your Blackstone!

Makes 4 Grilled Cheeses

Ingredients:

Cheese Mixture:

- ◀ 4 ounces (113 g) mascarpone cheese
- ◀ 4 ounces (113 g) cream cheese, at room temperature

French Toast Batter:

- ◀ 4 eggs
- ◀ 1 cup (240 ml) milk
- ◀ 2 teaspoons (10 ml) vanilla extract

Bananas Foster:

- ◀ 8 tablespoons (114 g) salted butter, divided
- ◀ 4 tablespoons (56 g) packed brown sugar
- ◀ 4 tablespoons (60 ml) banana liqueur or brandy
- ◀ 2 small bananas, thickly sliced

Assembling:

- ◀ 8 slices brioche bread
- ◀ Pinch of sea salt flakes

Instructions:

1. Start by mixing the mascarpone and cream cheese in a bowl until well combined. Set aside for later.

2. In a large shallow bowl, whisk together the eggs, milk, and vanilla to create the French toast batter. Stir until thoroughly mixed and then set aside.

3. Preheat the center of your griddle to medium heat. Melt 4 tablespoons (57 g) of butter in the center. Sprinkle the brown sugar over the melted butter and stir until it dissolves, about 2 to 3 minutes. Add the banana liqueur (or brandy) and bring the mixture to a simmer. Once it thickens, add the banana slices and stir for 1 to 2 minutes until well-coated. Remove the mixture from the heat and let it cool slightly. Use a splash of water to create steam and clean any sticky residue from the griddle. Then, lightly oil the griddle surface.

4. Evenly spread the mascarpone mixture on one side of each slice of bread. Top 4 slices with the banana mixture on the mascarpone side, adding a sprinkle of sea salt before placing the remaining slices on top, cheese side down. Soak each sandwich in the French toast batter for about 1 minute on each side.

5. In the same medium-heat area of the griddle, melt the remaining 4 tablespoons (57 g) of butter. Place the sandwiches on the griddle and cook for 3 to 4 minutes, or until the bottoms are golden brown. Flip the sandwiches and continue cooking for another 3 to 4 minutes until both sides are golden brown. Once cooked, remove the grilled cheeses from the griddle and let them rest for 2 minutes.

6. Enjoy this delightful twist on a classic sandwich!

Appendix 1: Measurement Conversion Chart

VOLUME EQUIVALENTS(DRY)

US STANDARD	METRIC (APPROXIMATE)
1/8 teaspoon	0.5 mL
1/4 teaspoon	1 mL
1/2 teaspoon	2 mL
3/4 teaspoon	4 mL
1 teaspoon	5 mL
1 tablespoon	15 mL
1/4 cup	59 mL
1/2 cup	118 mL
3/4 cup	177 mL
1 cup	235 mL
2 cups	475 mL
3 cups	700 mL
4 cups	1 L

VOLUME EQUIVALENTS(LIQUID)

US STANDARD	US STANDARD (OUNCES)	METRIC (APPROXIMATE)
2 tablespoons	1 fl.oz.	30 mL
1/4 cup	2 fl.oz.	60 mL
1/2 cup	4 fl.oz.	120 mL
1 cup	8 fl.oz.	240 mL
1 1/2 cup	12 fl.oz.	355 mL
2 cups or 1 pint	16 fl.oz.	475 mL
4 cups or 1 quart	32 fl.oz.	1 L
1 gallon	128 fl.oz.	4 L

WEIGHT EQUIVALENTS

US STANDARD	METRIC (APPROXIMATE)
1 ounce	28 g
2 ounces	57 g
5 ounces	142 g
10 ounces	284 g
15 ounces	425 g
16 ounces (1 pound)	455 g
1.5 pounds	680 g
2 pounds	907 g

TEMPERATURES EQUIVALENTS

FAHRENHEIT(F)	CELSIUS(C) (APPROXIMATE)
225 °F	107 °C
250 °F	120 °C
275 °F	135 °C
300 °F	150 °C
325 °F	160 °C
350 °F	180 °C
375 °F	190 °C
400 °F	205 °C
425 °F	220 °C
450 °F	235 °C
475 °F	245 °C
500 °F	260 °C

Appendix 2: Recipes Index